Understanding
WORLD
RELIGIONS
in 15 Minutes a Day

Understanding
WORLD
RELIGIONS
in 15 Minutes a Day

GARRY R. MORGAN

BETHANY HOUSE PUBLISHERS
a division of Baker Publishing Group
Minneapolis, Minnesota

© 2012 by Garry R. Morgan

Published by Bethany House Publishers
11400 Hampshire Avenue South
Bloomington, Minnesota 55438
www.bethanyhouse.com

Bethany House Publishers is a division of
Baker Publishing Group, Grand Rapids, Michigan

Printed in the United States of America

Library of Congress Cataloging-in-Publication Data
Morgan, Garry R.
    Understanding world religions in 15 minutes a day : learn the basics of
Islam, Buddhism, Hinduism, Mormonism, Christianity, and many more /
Garry R. Morgan.
        p. cm.
    Summary: "A professor of intercultural studies explores major world reli-
gions in 40 short chapters"—Provided by publisher.
    ISBN 978-0-7642-1003-7 (pbk. : alk. paper)
    1. Religions. I. Title.
BL80.3.M67 2012
200—dc23   2012013120

Scripture quotations are from the New American Standard Bible®, copyright © 1960, 1962, 1963, 1968, 1971, 1972, 1973, 1975, 1977, 1995 by The Lockman Foundation. Used by permission.

Cover design by Eric Walljasper

12   13   14   15   16   17   18   7   6   5   4   3   2   1

To my students
at Northwestern College:
Through teaching you,
I have learned much.

Contents

Contents

Preface

Today nearly six *billion* people profess some form of religion. Not only is there tremendous variety of religious beliefs, within any given religion there are disparities in some beliefs and practices. Add to this the cultural variations that impact any religion practiced in multiple parts of the world and a kaleidoscope of differences emerges.

The migration patterns of recent decades (over one billion people on the move since 1970) have brought previously isolated religious groups into contact with followers of other religions, or into new settings that have compelled some alteration of practices, resulting in even more changes. (This is not a new phenomenon in India, where Hindus, Muslims, Christians, Sikhs, Jains, Zoroastrians and Buddhists already have lived together for centuries.)

Trying to describe this vast religious array is challenging, since there are exceptions to almost anything one would say; trying to do so with brevity is even more difficult. It is my sincere hope that this book will bring clarity rather than confusion to those who may know little about religions outside (or including) their own. If you wish to know even more, I recommend Lewis Hopfe and Mark Woodward's *Religions of the World*, which I have used for many years in my World Religions courses. This college textbook is very readable and includes samples from the sacred texts of each religion covered.

At the publisher's request, this book intends to be descriptive rather than evaluative or polemic. It is designed to offer a concise overview of the major world religions and a sampling of some newer religious movements. Undoubtedly my own convictions have impacted my writing, but I have tried to be accurate and fair even when describing belief systems with which I personally disagree. Far too much contemporary writing by followers of one religion about others utilizes caricature and straw man arguments. My goal always is to be respectful.

Garry Morgan

March 2012

Acknowledgments

I wish to thank my wife, Connie, whose patience and encouragement kept me going in the writing of this book. I am grateful for my colleagues at Northwestern College who made allowances for my limited schedule during this period. And most of all, I give thanks to God, who demonstrated his grace to me in Jesus Christ and gave me a life filled with opportunities to interact with the followers of other faiths. To him be the glory.

What Is Religion?

Ask most people if they know what religion is and they will say yes. Ask them to define it, though, and you're likely to get blank stares and some mumbles. While we usually recognize religion when we see it, definitions are more challenging. Most people assume it has something to do with God, or gods, but that's not always the case. Definitions tend either to be so broad they're unhelpful or so specific they omit or overlook certain religions.

In addition, religion overlaps with philosophy. Confucius probably thought of himself as nonreligious, yet his philosophical principles have been incorporated into Chinese religions. Indeed, when a philosopher devoutly follows a particular religion, it can become impossible to distinguish between it and his philosophy. Søren Kierkegaard, a nineteenth-century Danish philosopher regarded as a father of existentialism, had a deep Christian faith and wrote profound theological works. Nevertheless, philosophy differs from religion in that it typically does not involve corporate practices like worship.

One far-reaching effect of cultural diversity on a global scale is that disparities, divergences, and discrepancies are not only interreligious but also intra-religious—that is, within the same religion in different areas. An Ethiopian Orthodox worship service bears little outward resemblance to an Ecuadorian Pentecostal service, yet both groups share core Christian beliefs.

Further, because religion significantly impacts our worldview, religious beliefs and practices are highly interconnected with culture. Indeed, as with the philosophical, discerning the cultural from the religious can range from challenging to undoable, so intertwined are they. What outsiders may view as religious practice, adherents may see as simply a cultural tradition. Traditional Chinese people clean ancestral graves each spring; Westerners tend to identify this as a religious practice, while the Chinese think of it in cultural terms. In the same way yet in reverse, some non-natives enjoy attending Native American powwows to watch the "cultural" dances, but to the cultural insider these dances have spiritual import.

The English word *religion* comes from the Latin *religio*, meaning "awe or fear of a god or spirit." Most religions do affirm a supernatural realm and include practices intended to worship or placate gods or spirits. But again, not all belief systems typically classified as "religions" entail the supernatural or even uphold its existence. Confucianism, Taoism, Theravada Buddhism, and Jainism are found in every world religions textbook yet are indifferent or agnostic on the reality of the supernatural, especially in any personal sense.

Even those who study religion professionally struggle to agree on a definition. The theologian Paul Tillich called it "that which is of ultimate concern"—perhaps an accurate descriptor but too general to be very useful as a definition. Anthropologist Michael Alan Park defines it as "a set of beliefs and behaviors pertaining to the supernatural." While most anthropological explanations insist on inclusion of the supernatural, Edward Norbeck says religion is a "distinctive symbolic expression of human life that interprets man himself and his universe, providing motives for human action" (in *Religion in Human Life* [1974:6]). William James said religion "consists of the belief that there is an unseen order, and that our supreme good lies in harmoniously adjusting ourselves thereto." Note that neither of these latter two necessitates affirmation of the supernatural.

Despite the variety, sifting through definitions does steer us toward helpful principles. First, one religion component is an organized system of beliefs. In some cases the organization may not be obvious to outsiders, but no religion is made up of random, unrelated creeds. Second, not all religions involve worship, but they do all mandate or at least commend certain behaviors and actions—corporate, individual, or both—that are related to the belief system. Third, a religion answers questions about the unknown.

What William James called an "unseen order" relates to how a religion answers what are usually termed *ultimate questions.* The various religions respond to these queries in an astonishing array of ways. Whether or not the answers are interwoven in a systematic manner, they guide people in thinking about what is beyond that which our five senses can perceive.

The foremost ultimate question is "What is ultimate reality?" For theists (primarily, adherents to Christianity, Judaism, Islam), the answer is God. Buddhists say the answer is Nothing (specifically, a void, or Nirvana). Secular Humanists say it's the material universe, beyond which nothing else exists.

The next question is "What is the nature of the universe?" Theists maintain that God created it. Secular Humanists believe the universe (or the material components that comprise it) is eternal and has no beginning or creator (First Cause). Hindus say the material universe is an illusion; we think it's

15

real, but it doesn't actually exist—rather, all reality is spiritual in nature.

Other questions asked:

"What does it mean to be human?"

"What is humanity's primary problem?"

"What happens after death?"

From one religion to another, the answers vary as much as their outward practices. Clearly, all religions are not basically the same.

In summary, there is no single right answer to defining *religion*. For this book we'll use this working definition: "Religion is an organized system of beliefs that answers ultimate questions and commends certain actions or behaviors based on the answers to those questions."

An Extra Minute

Is Secular Humanism a religion?

Academic textbooks do not include it among the religions studied. Books that Christians write on world religions normally do include a chapter on secularism or atheism (though these are not exactly the same thing).

Why the difference?

Secular Humanists are vociferously opposed to being considered a religion, largely because most people assume religion involves belief in the supernatural. State universities won't buy textbooks over the objections of Secular Humanists.

However, like Confucianism, Taoism, Jainism, and other nontheistic belief systems included in academic textbooks, Secular Humanism fits our working definition, has significant impact on today's world, and serves functionally as a religion. For consistency, this book includes a chapter on it.

Why Learn About Other Religions?

In many parts of the world, people once lived their entire lives without even meeting a follower of another religion. Today, globalization, fueled by migration, politics, economics, and the Internet, has brought awareness of other faiths to most of earth's population. Understanding the "global village" is impossible without some grasp of the religious beliefs that shape people's behaviors, attitudes, and actions.

Religion is called a cultural universal because it is found in all human societies. Even secular anthropologists acknowledge that no culture has yet been found that does not have some form of religion. This universality suggests that knowing something about this topic is crucial to comprehending humanity. Even though the nonreligious today number in the hundreds of millions, the vast majority professes belonging to some form of religious system. To fathom the *why* of what people do and say, again, one must understand the religious beliefs that shape their worldviews.

The variety of belief and practice on the globe now is astounding. The frequently heard statement "All religions are basically the same" is based on the superficial observation that religion seems to be about guiding and motivating people to "behave well." However, no one who has learned what adherents to the various religions actually believe and practice would make such a comment. There isn't even common ground in another common misconception: "All religions are just different paths to God." Religious belief is as much about the nature of God (or gods, goddesses, spirits, or other powers) as it is about how to reach or interact with this deity. In fact, many religions aren't trying to reach any deity at all.

Again, there is significant variety within each of the world's religions. Christianity has many denominations (with new ones springing up every year), and it is by no means unique in having multiple groups, often with significant disparities in belief and practice. For example, just knowing that a person is a Buddhist tells you relatively little about what he believes, as Buddhism has three major divisions, each with multiple and significantly different subgroups.

Further, international politics today is impossible to understand without some knowledge of religion. Friction between countries develops because governments make decisions without considering the religious beliefs of other nations. News media and foreign policy experts try to explain terrorism without knowing or grasping the religious beliefs of those involved (and founding or supporting terroristic groups is not limited to one religion). We may support one side or the other in the Israeli-Palestinian conflict because of assumptions about religion. To be sure, religion is not the only factor impacting global political events, but it is a big one. In most of the world, people don't dichotomize the sacred and the secular as we commonly do in the West, so elsewhere religious considerations are much more at the forefront of people's minds in assessing political issues.

Also, religion has been the motivation for, and provider of, content for much of the world's art and music. Imagine, for example, trying to understand Handel's *Messiah* with no knowledge of Christianity, or Indian art without a grasp of Hinduism. Ancient dramas and countless more-recent plays and films draw upon themes that require some knowledge of religion to comprehend. Literature of all ages makes reference to religious themes and practices.

Some people's belief includes a form of "If it's God's [or the gods'] will for life to be better, it will get better without our efforts; if it's not, things won't improve no matter what we do." If a society's religious basis includes a fatalistic worldview, then motivating its people to implement policies and adopt behaviors that would tangibly benefit them can be challenging. In animistic societies, people may fear making changes lest they anger the spirits who can bring disease, crop failures, or other calamities upon the community. We need to understand religious convictions in order to be effective in matters of economics and development.

Migration has brought refugees and new immigrants to communities far from their homelands, affecting not only major cities but smaller rural areas as well. In many cases, these arrivals espouse religions different from those of the communities where they settle. (Two examples involving where I live are the many animistic Hmong making their home in Minnesota and in central California and the Somali Muslims who have settled in Minnesota and Toronto.) Knowing something about their religions is essential to interacting and communicating with them meaningfully.

It isn't unusual in today's world to compare the best of one's own faith to the worst of another. This is neither honest nor respectful. Comparisons must be accurate and must consider the whole of a religion's teaching and practice. This book endeavors to present each religion in a straightforward way, so that a reader who is a follower while perhaps disagreeing with certain assessments, would say the description is truthful and fair.

An Extra Minute

Followers of different faiths sometimes use the same words but intend very different meanings, which can lead to confusion. For Christians, being "born again" is a positive statement about spiritual life, taken from Jesus' words in John 3. To Hindus, it implies reincarnation, which they are trying to escape. So when a Christian asks a Hindu about being reborn, the likely response is, "I've already been born again and again and again. That's what I want to get away from." We need to (1) find out what people actually believe and (2) not assume words mean the same thing in every context.

Christianity:
What Sets It Apart?

"C hristianity isn't a religion, it's a relationship!" We often hear this when someone's trying to set Christianity apart from "religion." Is it accurate? Is this the characteristic that makes Christianity unique? And if not, what does?

Based on our description of religion from chapter 1, Christianity clearly fits the definition. It is an organized system of belief and practice that answers ultimate questions and guides daily life. But why have we come to think of *religion* as a negative term in the first place?

Due to historical abuses, we tend to view it as something artificial or without true meaning. However, the New Testament uses the term in James 1:27 with the adjectives *pure* and *undefiled*. Religion *can* become tradition without meaning, yet that isn't the fault of religion itself—responsibility would belong with those who wrongly practice a given faith.

So believers could say that Christianity is the religious expression of our relationship with Jesus Christ. Our faith uses the Bible to answer ultimate questions about God and life. Because the Christian's relationship with God through Christ is lived out with other followers of Jesus (what the New Testament calls "the body of Christ"), we worship and engage in other activities as a unified group, and this also is what characterizes religion.

Also, regarding the "religion vs. relationship" debate, we should keep in mind that other religious systems claim a relationship with the god or gods they revere and worship. The Qur'an says, "God is nearer [to a man] than [his] jugular vein" (50:16). The Bhagavad Gita describes an incarnation of the god Krishna who helps a warrior king make significant life decisions. Many animists maintain relationships with ancestral spirits.

If relationship itself is not what makes Christianity unique, what does? Starting with stating the obvious, Jesus of Nazareth is the most compelling religious figure of all time. Historians, scholars, and even leaders of other religions widely acknowledge and admire (although sometimes distort) the unique quality of his life and teachings.

For the Christian, however, it is not Jesus' teachings or even his earthly life that are most important. We look to Jesus not just as a gifted teacher and moral example but as our Savior. His death and resurrection are the watershed events that stand at the center of our faith. By them, Jesus established the truth of his claim to be God's unique Son—fully human and fully divine—and provided the means of salvation for humankind, separated from God by sin.

Another way to describe the faith's uniqueness is with the word *grace*. Grace means giving someone something they don't deserve. Because the God of the Bible is a God of grace, he takes the first step to repair our relationship with him after disobedience (sin). Because of grace, God provides the way of salvation in Jesus, who takes our punishment for wrongdoing. Because of grace, God can be both just (punishing sin) and forgiving (removing sin).

All other religious systems believe the main responsibility for solving life's problems rests upon people. Christianity reveals and demonstrates that we cannot set things right by our own efforts, which makes grace all the more astounding and precious.

Historically, the Christian church is widely regarded to have begun on the day of Pentecost (described in Acts 2). It spread widely and grew quickly over the next several centuries. Early on, even as seen within the pages of the New Testament, it began developing religious forms. Initially, these were heavily influenced by Judaism. The first Christians worshiped in the Jewish temple in Jerusalem and used the Hebrew Scriptures we now call the Old Testament.

But as non-Jews accepted the Christian message (the gospel) and became followers of Jesus, the church began adopting Hellenistic (Greek) forms, especially in how the message of Jesus was explained to others. John's gospel, for example, describes Jesus as the *Logos* (Word), a term with significant meaning to those influenced by Greek philosophy.

Indeed, Christianity can flourish in any culture. The New Testament focuses more on principles for living and the type of people we're supposed to be (i.e., character qualities) than on specific behaviors, so its practices and forms tend to take on the local flavor of surrounding cultures. For example, the apostle Paul commands husbands to love their wives (Ephesians 5:25); the specific ways Christians obey this order look different from culture to culture.

This flexibility, coupled with extensive geographic expansion, political issues (especially after Christianity received favored status from the Roman Empire in the late fourth century), and theological differences of opinion, eventually led to divisions.

The Western church, centered in Rome, became what is now the Roman Catholic Church. The Eastern church, based in Constantinople, became the (Eastern) Orthodox Church with its regional fellowships (Greek Orthodox, Russian Orthodox, etc.).

Later, near the end of the fifteenth century, various reformers protested against abuses within the Catholic Church. Martin Luther, John Calvin, and others, largely after being excommunicated, organized new expressions of the Christian faith that came to be known as Protestant churches. While there are smaller branches on the Christian church tree, Roman Catholic, Orthodox, and Protestant form the largest or primary three.

From AD 500, and for more than a millennium, the Christian message was largely spread by groups of Catholic monks, reaching eastward as far as Japan and west to the New World. By the eighteenth century, Protestants began what came to be called the modern missionary movement, taking the gospel to every part of the world. Today, Christianity truly is a global faith. While there are still areas and people groups that have not heard the name of Jesus Christ, he has followers in virtually every country.

An Extra Minute

Christians of all walks comprise about a third of the world's population (about 2.1 billion in 2010). Approximately 1.1 billion belong to the Roman Catholic Church, about 600 million to Protestant churches, and about 270 million are Eastern Orthodox, with the balance in independent groups. In 1900, about 68 percent of the world's Christians lived on the European continent, with about 14 percent in North America. By 2050, Africa is likely to have about 29 percent of the world's Christians, followed by Asia with 20 percent. Church historians refer to this trend as Christianity's "global center" shifting from north to south.

Roman Catholic Christianity

The first Christians had little organizational structure. Although local churches all around the Mediterranean world were in contact and even cooperated in activities (like sending support to Paul's missionary team or providing financial assistance to the Jerusalem church during a famine), there was no central human authority.

The *apostles* were a chosen group who established new churches and provided special guidance during the New Testament era. These men, primarily Peter and James in Jerusalem, and Paul, the church planter, were looked to for wisdom and advice on matters of doctrine and practice (e.g., see Acts 15 or Paul's *epistles*—letters written to many of the local churches). However, the local assembly of believers in each city believed they drew their authority directly from Jesus Christ, led by the Scriptures and his Holy Spirit.

The New Testament describes three types of church leaders, always in connection with a given congregation. The first have traditionally been called *bishops*. The literal translation of the

Greek word is "overseer," which clearly describes their role. The second, *elders*, were responsible for teaching, leading, and spiritual care. *Deacons* primarily provided material care for the congregation, though their qualifications were similar to elders and many, like Stephen, the first Christian martyr, were gifted preachers and teachers (see Acts 6). It seems likely there were also *deaconesses*. While their exact title is not certain, Paul mentions by name a number of women who served in a ministry capacity.

This decentralized leadership aided the church's survival through the waves of persecution it faced during its first three centuries. By the time the last of the apostles died (c. AD 90), each city where believers gathered had a bishop or overseer. Church buildings weren't common for several centuries; groups of believers met in homes, usually with an elder present, while large, corporate gatherings were held outside or in rented facilities.

Many bishops, especially in the larger cities, were gifted theologians, speakers, and writers—two of the better known are Athanasius and Augustine, both from North Africa. The writings of these and other influential bishops were circulated as the church refined ways of stating New Testament truths in doctrinal statements and dealt with questions and controversies that came up over the years in specific contexts.

Persecution during the first three centuries was sporadic and sometimes localized. Begun initially by Jewish leaders, after Jerusalem's fall (AD 70), the Romans became the persecutors. The most severe and widespread wave came under Emperor Diocletian (ruled AD 284–305). His successor, Constantine, abruptly reversed policy (through the Edict of Milan, AD 313) and granted Christianity legal status equal to all other religions in the empire.

Constantine took two other actions that significantly shaped Christianity. In 325, he called the Council of Nicaea, to be held in present-day Turkey, inviting 1,800 bishops from all over the empire to discuss and settle questions regarding the nature of Christ. Several hundred were able to attend, and they produced the Nicene Creed, still used in some worship services today.

Then in 330, Constantine moved his political capital from Rome to Byzantium, which was renamed Constantinople (now Istanbul, Turkey). In the western part of the empire, the church filled the political vacuum. The bishop in Rome already held great prestige and influence over the rest of the church, and although the New Testament doesn't mention it, there's a church tradition that says the apostle Peter traveled there and became its first bishop.

This influence, increasing significantly after 330, also brought increased conflict with Christianity's eastern branch, which resisted the Roman bishop's claim to lead all Christians. Geography, politics, and theological differences all led to a gradual and often acrimonious separation that became complete in 1204, when Crusaders from the west, en route to the Holy Land, attacked and looted Constantinople.

Within a century, the Christian church went from persecuted minority to appointing emperors and running political systems. After the Empire's collapse, the church became the unifying force in Europe. But with more political influence came declining spiritual fervor. In response, monastic orders were formed by those who wanted to focus on the spiritual aspects of Christianity. Yet the monks did not simply withdraw from society. They taught the people in their areas, maintained centers of learning, and sent missionaries to other parts of the world.

Early in the Middle Ages (roughly AD 500–1500), the bishop of Rome became the recognized head of the Western church and was called the pope. He claimed authority over all Christians, and thus the church came to be called the *Catholic* Church, meaning "all-embracing" or universal. It was not until the Reformation, when some Christian groups broke away from the

27

pope's authority, that *Roman Catholic* came to describe the section of the church that recognized papal leadership. Today, Christianity is described as having three major branches: Roman Catholic, Protestant, and Eastern Orthodox.

The Reformation produced an often violent reaction (the Counter-Reformation) from the Catholic Church but also brought some positive changes. Over time, the pope's amassing of power and wealth had led to corruption and other outrages. The Council of Trent (1545) was an effort to stem the tide of Christians leaving the Catholic Church to join the Reformers.

The sale of indulgences and other abuses were restrained, but certain doctrines were formulated to specifically "counter" Reformation beliefs and establish the claim to be the only true and legitimate form of Christianity. Opposing Protestant trust in the Bible's sole authority, the Council stated that church tradition carried equal weight. Protestants promoted translating the Bible into common languages and providing it to all believers (with help from the recently invented printing press); the Council maintained that the Latin Bible was the only true Scripture, and only the Catholic Church could interpret it.

Although some new *dogmas* (official statements of belief) were added over the centuries, the doctrines established by Trent defined Roman Catholic Christianity until the middle of the twentieth century. The First Vatican Council (Vatican I, 1869) had added the dogma of *papal infallibility*: that the pope's official pronouncements (*ex cathedra*) are without error. In 1962, Pope John XXIII called the Second Vatican Council (Vatican II), which met until 1965, and wrought momentous change. Best known for replacing Latin with vernacular languages in the mass, it also recognized Protestant and Orthodox believers as true Christians and allowed ordinary members to read the Bible for themselves. Today, the Roman Catholic Church, with 1.1 billion members globally, remains the largest Christian branch.

An Extra Minute

The organizational structure of the Roman Catholic Church is often used as a model in business management courses because of its "flatness," that is, minimal layers from top to bottom. With more than a billion members, there are only six layers from pope to ordinary member (layperson). In between are the offices of cardinal, archbishop, bishop, and priest.

Eastern Orthodox Christianity

Eastern Orthodoxy, the smallest of Christianity's three major branches and perhaps the least-known by other Christians, has its geographic roots in the Middle East, where the faith began. As it spread, Orthodox Christianity developed regional variations, although most share similar beliefs and practices. Today, it remains dominant in Greece, Russia, and Romania (among other countries) and is the most common form of Christianity in Muslim-majority countries like Egypt and Turkey.

Due to cultural and political differences, the Eastern Orthodox Church quickly developed differences with the Western form that became the Roman Catholic Church. It tended to be more contemplative; the Western church was more pragmatic. Although very much integrated into political life, especially during the Byzantine period, Eastern Christianity did not develop the Roman Church's secular power. In fact, emperors tended to have influence over the running of the church, whereas the reverse was true in Rome.

Furthermore, after the seventh century, much of the Eastern Orthodox Church came under the political domination of Muslim rulers as Islam spread westward, and this influenced its theology and practice. Although the Western church lost territory to Islam in North Africa and Spain, Charles Martel's decisive victory at the Battle of Tours (732) kept most of Europe in Christian hands.

In chapter 3, we discussed other key historical and political factors that led to schism between the Western (Roman Catholic) and Eastern (Orthodox) branches; there were theological elements, too. Because it produced some of the early church's most influential theologians and writers, the East resented the insistence that Rome have the final say in all matters. This unwillingness to bow to the pope's authority was at the heart of this growing divide.

One early theological controversy had to do with understanding relationships within the Trinity. Both branches agreed that God is one being who has existed eternally as three persons, Father, Son, and Spirit. Both rejected polytheism and modalism, the heretical idea that God originally manifested himself as the Father, then became the Son, and now is the Holy Spirit. But the Western church held that the Spirit "proceeded from both the Father and the Son," while the Eastern branch took Jesus' words in John's gospel about the Father sending the Spirit to mean that he "proceeded [only] from the Father."

More widely familiar was what has come to be called the "Iconoclastic Controversy." The Western church used statues of Jesus, Mary, and many saints in their worship. To the Eastern church, this was idolatrous, in violation of the second commandment (to have no graven image). They developed a two-dimensional art form called the *icon*, a picture for use in worship and prayer.

Before the final split in 1054, the Western church insisted on celibacy for priests, while marriage was permitted in the East.

31

The West baptized infants by sprinkling; the East baptized infants by immersion. The West began giving laypeople only bread during Communion, whereas the laity in the East continued to receive both bread and wine.

Language was important in how the two branches spread and developed. The West used Latin for worship and resisted further translation of the Bible into other tongues. The East used Greek and promoted translation of God's Word into the vernacular. The Orthodox monk Cyril developed an alphabet for the Slavic languages that bears his name; Cyrillic orthography is used today for Russian, Polish, Czech, and Bulgarian, among other languages.

Through the missionary work of dedicated monks, Eastern Christianity spread from the Middle East into Eastern Europe and northward into Russia, as well as into what is now Iraq and Iran. By the close of the first millennium, geographic expansion slowed and eventually halted. Leading up to and into the twentieth century, Eastern European and Russian immigrants brought the Orthodox faith to Australia and North America. Today, 270 million Eastern Orthodox members are organized into fellowships of independent churches, usually by country, including Greek Orthodox, Russian Orthodox, and the Orthodox Church in America, each with its own synod of bishops. The Ecumenical Patriarch of Constantinople is given the honor of "first among equals" and holds significant influence but does not have the power or authority that the pope has over the Roman Catholic Church.

The Eastern Orthodox Church is also officially known as the Orthodox Catholic Church. Similar to but separate from the Eastern Orthodox Church is the Oriental Orthodox Church (though *oriental* means "eastern"), which includes the Egyptian Coptic Church, the Ethiopian Orthodox Church, and several smaller groups. These differ from Eastern Orthodoxy in that they accept only the first three of seven ecumenical councils that Eastern Orthodoxy considers to be the definitive interpretation of Scripture for belief and practice.

The Oriental Orthodox churches are of ancient origin. The Coptic Church traces its beginnings to Mark the Evangelist, while the Ethiopian Orthodox Church traces to the return of the eunuch who encountered Philip, in Acts 8. These churches refused the conclusions of the Council of Chalcedon (451) and broke away prior to the East-West split (1054). *Note:* The Orthodox Church of Alexandria, in Egypt, is part of Eastern (not Oriental) Orthodoxy.

An Extra Minute

How does the name *Orthodox* differ from the term *orthodox*? The term comes from two Greek words literally rendered *right belief*. So the term *orthodox* means believing in line with accepted Christian teaching (as opposed to *heresy*, wrong belief). Any right-believing Christian is orthodox. The Eastern Church adopted the word into their name in the conviction that their belief was correct.

Protestant Christianity

Protestant is an umbrella term generally used to describe a vast variety of churches that are neither Roman Catholic nor Eastern Orthodox. The name comes from the "protests" by Martin Luther, John Calvin, and many others against abuses of power and some doctrines in the Roman Catholic Church. The Reformers were people of the fourteenth through the seventeenth centuries who sought to bring change to Christianity in Europe. Their writings continue to exert substantial influence over hundreds of millions of believers today.

Historically, the Protestant Reformation began as an attempt to, as the word implies, *reform* Christianity. Luther and the others saw their efforts not as bringing anything new to the faith but as restoring biblical teaching and practice established prior to the development of Rome's papal system. They didn't intend initially to form a new church organization—they did so only after they were excommunicated (removed from membership) and threatened with death by the Catholic Church hierarchy.

The congregations that followed the Reformers became the Protestant churches.

That the word *reformed* is utilized in countless ways today can be confusing. The Reformation period produced several organizations. The churches following Luther's teaching and leadership came to be called Lutheran, while those that followed Calvin were called Reformed, even though both were part of the Reformation and are relatively similar in doctrine. Over time, the Reformed churches subdivided, usually along national lines, into many denominations (e.g., the Dutch Reformed Church, the Reformed Church of America). Calvin's doctrines, with additions by a number of others, came to be called Reformed Theology, best known for its doctrine of God's sovereignty, especially in *election,* God's choosing of who will be saved. Over the years, newer denominations, notably the Presbyterians and many Baptist groups, embraced most of Calvin's "reformed" doctrines, while disagreeing with some beliefs and practices of the Reformed Church.

Historically, two core issues framed the Protestant disagreement with Catholicism. The first concerns *salvation,* the way in which a person avoids God's righteous judgment on the sinful nature and is reconciled into right relationship with him. Protestants insist that the Bible clearly states salvation is "by grace alone, through faith alone, in Jesus Christ alone," in contrast to a combination of grace and good works. The second, *Sola Scriptura,* is the belief that the Bible is the final authority for determining doctrine and practice rather than a combination of Scripture and tradition. Additional areas of divergence grew over time as Protestant leaders refined and developed their doctrines.

The various Protestant churches survived Roman Catholic attempts to exterminate them, in part because many European political leaders saw in them the chance to escape papal oppression and attain greater regional autonomy. Ultimately,

35

Protestants contributed considerably to the rise of nationalism and the development of today's European countries. This association developed into the state church system, in which a whole country officially recognized just one denomination (e.g., the Lutheran Church in Sweden or Norway).

Unfortunately, this also led to a number of wars, both civil (within one country) and between Catholic and Protestant countries. Some nations were tolerant of those whose beliefs were not in step with the state church, such as Holland, which, although officially Dutch Reformed, became a haven for persecuted Christians from France, England, and elsewhere (such as the Pilgrims who later settled Plymouth Colony in North America). Elsewhere, persecution of dissenters ranged from moderate to severe. In some Protestant countries, Catholics were persecuted, and many Protestants were killed in France and other Catholic countries.

Persecution extended even to other Protestants of the "wrong" variety. The Baptist pastor John Bunyan, author of *Pilgrim's Progress*, spent much of his adult life in prison for refusal to "conform" to the Anglican Church.

New denominations proliferated as Protestant Christianity spread across Europe and then into North America. Beginning in the nineteenth century, the changes reached Africa and Asia. Without the central leadership authority that characterizes the Catholic Church, formation of new organizations is much easier. Sometimes these groups began because of doctrinal disputes. For example, Freewill Baptists in England split from the majority of Baptists (who theologically were closer to the Reformed Church). Some developed due to geography and politics. After American independence, for instance, Presbyterians in the U.S. chose independence from their Scottish origins. Baptists and many other American denominations split over slavery (it has been argued that this was more a doctrinal dispute than a political one).

Spiritual revival has also led to the creation of denominations. The Azusa Street Revival of 1906, for example, led to the formation of the Apostolic Faith Movement, the Assemblies of God, and many other Pentecostal groups. Sometimes new groups form because of conflict of personality or conviction between leaders.

The twentieth-century Ecumenical Movement attempted to reverse the trend of proliferation with the goal of merging Protestants into one organizational structure. They've seen limited success with the United and Uniting Churches in Canada and Australia respectively; in both countries Methodists, Presbyterians, and Congregationalists merged into one organization. The movement has had more success encouraging cooperation between denominations through the World Council of Churches and its national affiliates than in bringing about organizational mergers and a reduction in the number of denominations.

An Extra Minute

How many Protestant denominations are there? The diversity and geographic expansion of Protestant Christianity makes counting difficult. There are more than fifty different Baptist groups just in the U.S., where the largest, the Southern Baptist Convention, has more than sixteen million members. Adding to the complications is globalization: If missionaries of one denomination in one country start new churches in another country and those churches form an association, is that a new denomination or part of the original? They are usually independent (though related) organizations, but not always. At the beginning of the twenty-first century, renowned researcher David Barrett counted 33,830 Protestant denominations globally (in *World Christian Encyclopedia*).

Evangelical Christianity

*E*vangelicalism is a movement in Protestant Christianity that began in the twentieth century as a response to changes in the beliefs, or doctrines, of some Protestant churches, especially with regard to the Bible's authority.

Modernism, and more recently postmodernism, have influenced the thinking of many and cast doubt in their minds about some scriptural teachings. While there is a broad range of belief within Protestantism, some see the Bible as an ancient, error-filled human record of religious experience rather than a divinely inspired revelation from God. As a result, they reject one or more foundational doctrines of the Christian faith.

For example, some dismiss "Jesus as the only way to salvation" as arrogance. Some consider the need for salvation at all from "God's wrath" to be an abhorrent myth. They might say Jesus is a remarkable human teacher, but not the divine-human Son of God. They deny his miracles and his resurrection and, in the extreme, question whether he actually existed as a historical person. And, despite all these denials of historic orthodoxy, many who hold these beliefs still consider themselves Christian and remain active in churches and seminaries. They find the content of Jesus' teaching to be mostly a useful source of principles for right living.

Catholicism has been impacted by the same philosophical and worldview trends, and many today, including some leaders, hold one or more of the above beliefs. Certainly this has brought dissension and debate into Catholic scholarship and writing. Unlike some Protestant denominations, though, the Roman Church's official teachings still reflect a more traditional stance with regard to the life, death, and resurrection of Jesus Christ.

How did these changes come about? In seventeenth-century Europe, new ways of thinking produced what is now called the Enlightenment. One key Enlightenment facet was its emphasis on rationalism, the elevation of human reason in determining truth. If something could not be understood by the human mind, it was rejected as false.

There were positive aspects to rationalism—e.g., development of the scientific method—but it also rejected revealed religion and made humankind the ultimate authority. By the eighteenth century, a different way of studying the Scriptures emerged. Biblical accounts of miracles were assumed to be fictitious, since Europeans of that era couldn't produce miracles themselves. Biblical statements about Jesus' deity and resurrection were dismissed as the fabrications of "primitive" human minds in the ancient world. The worldview that evolved from these ideas was called modernism. The macroevolutionary hypotheses brought forth by Charles Darwin's theories further influenced modernism's focus on the material world and rejection of the supernatural.

Initially, these humanistic ideas were limited to the educated elite and had little impact on the masses of European and North American Christians. But theological education would come to be influenced by modernistic views, and some Christian leaders became convinced that the church needed to change or else the faith would become irrelevant and die out. This process, over several decades, led some entire denominations to alter their doctrinal statements toward a modernist viewpoint.

The reaction by those who still believed in the Bible as God's authoritative Word was strong. Dozens of new denominations were formed as churches split over belief in Jesus' virgin birth, miracles, and resurrection. By the 1920s, the labels *liberal* and *fundamentalist* were used to identify these two Christian groups. As modernist teachings grew in long-established seminaries, fundamentalists (so-called because they held to the "fundamentals" of biblical Christianity) started a number of Bible schools around the United States.

By the mid-1940s, fundamentalists had become increasingly disengaged from American society, separating themselves even from other Christians who did not believe exactly the same way. Some within fundamentalism became uncomfortable with this rigidity and negativism (fundamentalists, it was said, "were known more for what they were against than what they were for"). While still holding to biblical fundamentals regarding Christ's person and work, this new movement sought increased cooperation with other Christians, engaged in the pursuit of scholarship (the fundamentalist movement had become strongly anti-intellectual), and generally became more involved in society. Those within this group came to be known as evangelicals.

Today, *evangelical* has become an umbrella term for Christians who believe in the Bible's accuracy (the theological term is *inerrancy*) and full authority. They also believe in the necessity of being *born again* for salvation (see John 3).

The term is used broadly. It may describe an individual, a local church, or an entire denomination. It's used to identify subgroups within larger denominations, like the "evangelical wing" of the global Anglican Church. There are evangelical organizations, such as the Evangelical Theological Society. The World Evangelical Alliance is made up of more than a hundred national evangelical associations representing thousands of denominations, hundreds of thousands of churches, and approximately four hundred million Christians.

As the movement has grown, it's become more diverse nationally, ethnically, and culturally. Since modernist or liberal churches no longer believed in the necessity of faith in Christ for salvation, most twentieth-century missionary work was carried out by evangelicals. Although Pentecostal Christianity had earlier and different origins and for decades remained separate from evangelicalism, the two are often considered part of the same branch of Christianity. Now almost all non-biological growth in Christianity, globally, is in the evangelical-Pentecostal wing.

An Extra Minute

What's in a label? Terms can be perplexing. In contrast to *liberal* Christians, evangelicals are often labeled *conservative*. But *liberal* may refer to politics as well as theology, or it may mean a person is generous. Someone who's theologically liberal may be politically conservative, and vice versa. Denominations that generally have liberal theology in the sense described above are also known as conciliar, mainline Protestant, and ecumenical. Denominational labels aren't always reliable guides either. For example, some Presbyterian denominations are conciliar/liberal and others are evangelical/conservative. And despite the name, the Evangelical Lutheran Church of America, the largest Lutheran denomination in the U.S., *isn't* evangelical, doctrinally speaking (there are individual ELCA churches that hold evangelical views). It's more reliable to listen with discernment to the preaching and teaching of a local church than to go by any label.

Animism and Folk Religions

Animism, from the Latin *anima*, meaning "breath" or "spirit," is an umbrella term for a global family of thousands of religions. In textbooks, they're often called "basic religions," based on the evolutionary assumption that in human development animistic religions came first, then polytheistic, followed eventually by monotheistic (and today by atheistic). They're also known as traditional religions, since many followers see their practices as cultural traditions, in contrast to more formally organized faiths (e.g., Christianity, Islam). These religions rarely have written scriptures or sacred writings; beliefs and practices are passed along orally from one generation to the next.

The label *tribal religions* represents two features: First, the cultural groups most commonly thought of as practicing animistic religion are remote tribes that still have minimal contact with the rest of the world (such as South American Indian tribes in the Amazon jungles, or the isolated tribes of Papua New Guinea). Second, each group sees their religious beliefs and practices as exclusive to their own tribe. There is no thought that other people from different cultural groups ought to believe in the same spirits they serve.

However, the idea that only tribal groups practice animistic religion is a common mistake. *Folk religion* describes animistic beliefs and practices that are adapted into one of the formal world religions. Examples include spiritism in Brazilian Catholicism, Muslim prayers offered at the tombs of sheiks and martyrs, and the occult practices of Tibetan Buddhism.

In fact, all major religions have some followers who practice animistic rituals alongside formal activities. These may happen undercover, when the formal religion prohibits such activities, or they may be incorporated into the formal structure and ritual in a process called *syncretism*. Folk religion has a significant impact on billions of people who self-identify with Christianity, Hinduism, Islam, or one of the other major religions. Additionally, many New Age religions, although typically based on the Hindu concepts of karma and reincarnation, also include beliefs and practices related to animism, as do the rapidly growing Neopagan religions.

The animistic belief system is phenomenally pervasive; conservatively, 40 percent of the earth's population holds some form of animistic belief. Some textbooks just a half century ago predicted the dying out of animistic religions by the year 2000, as Western-style education progressed in developing nations. In actuality, there has been a resurgence of interest in this manner of connecting or dealing with the spirit world.

Not even the modernized West is exempt. Some Americans who profess to be Christian and attend church regularly believe the number thirteen is unlucky, won't walk under ladders, and seek four-leaf clovers for good luck. These practices are vestiges of European, pre-Christian animism.

How could such a vast variety of religious expression ever be joined together under one label? Well, despite tremendous differences in outward form, all animistic groups share certain common beliefs about the nature of the world. Animists believe the world is filled with spiritual powers. These may be personal spirit beings, such as ancestral spirits or nature-dwelling spirits. They may be impersonal forces, like Fate or the Evil Eye. Often it is a combination of several or all of these. These spiritual forces are believed to have influence, if not outright control, over people and events. Therefore, the animist's goal is to find out what spirits or forces are at work so that steps can be taken to protect oneself from harm and harness spiritual power for one's benefit. Manipulating the spirit world to obtain power or influence is at the core of this worldview.

Many educated people today, even religious ones, deride animistic beliefs as mere superstition, which implies that the spirit world isn't real. However, the scriptures of the formal world religions, including the Bible, acknowledge the reality of spiritual powers. Denial of the spiritual realm comes out of a rationalistic mindset, not formal religious belief.

Most animistic religions acknowledge the existence of a high creator god, but he is considered to be distant and unapproachable, perhaps even aloof to humans and their problems. It is the spirits that are near, active, and involved, and thus they must be dealt with to avoid or repair calamity and to gain power for achieving goals. Unlike the Holy Spirit of the Christian faith, these spirits are not considered to be God (or equal to God).

Though some of these beings are believed to be the spirits of recently departed ancestors, they're rarely regarded as benevolent or loving toward humans. At best, they're neutral; they may even be considered malevolent. Although believers may sometimes approach spirits proactively for help with life issues (e.g., doing well on a test or getting a job), most animistic rituals are in response to a problem (e.g., illness or drought), and involve divining which spirit or spirits are causing the particular calamity so that they can be appeased and convinced to stop causing the issue. In some cases, the ritual might involve calling on a stronger spirit to drive out a weaker spirit.

Animistic religions are generally pragmatic in the sense of focusing on the here-and-now; daily life matters more than eternal destiny or life after death. When an animistic culture has adopted a formal religion, a parallel form of religious practice is common. People claim to be Christian or Muslim and attend church or mosque for matters of the next life, but retain animistic rituals to deal with matters of this life.

The next two chapters are more detailed looks at two animistic groupings: Native American religions and African Traditional religions.

An Extra Minute

Some people incorrectly use the word *pagan* to refer to a non-religious person. Historically, and conversely, *Paganism* was the name given to the ancient European animistic (in some cases, polytheistic) religions preceding the arrival of Christianity from the Middle East. Neopaganism is now a growing movement that seeks to revive these religions with something of a New Age twist. Some practitioners aim to accurately restore the old traditions to look and be just as they were in the past; others are more eclectic and advocate reconstruction. Either way, a pagan is a *religious* person.

Native American Religions

L ike all animistic religions, Native American religions (NARs) provide a variety of beliefs and practices that make generalizations challenging. Thus it is necessary to speak in the plural of Native religions. Depending on where they have settled, the various Native American people groups, or tribes, have made their living through agriculture, pastoral tending of livestock, or hunting and gathering. Some have lived in settled towns or small cities. Others have lived nomadically, following herds of buffalo or other wild game. One consequence has been an assortment of religious expressions and rituals.

Another factor inhibiting description of these religions is that in most cases Native Americans left no written records of life before the arrival of European immigrants. Written sources, therefore, usually have been produced by outside observers of Native life, which inserts a non-Native worldview into depictions and explanations, even when the writer strives to avoid bias. Many early sources, unfortunately, did not even attempt neutrality but describe these religions in negative terms.

Finally, Native American interactions with European settlers from the seventeenth century onward resulted in extensive conversion, at least outwardly, to Christianity. By the mid-twentieth century, most Native people professed to be Christian, though many mixed traditional practices with their new faith. Since 1960, there has been a massive resurgence of interest in Native culture and religions, with a subsequent reversal of the number of Native Americans professing Christianity. However, we cannot always know whether today's post-Christian Native practices and rituals are the same as they were before interaction with Europeans.

One applicable generalization is that NARs have a strong emphasis on the spirit world, something they share with the rest of the huge animistic category. But specific beliefs about its traits vary. Some Native tribes have worship rituals of key spirits such as Mother Earth, thunder and/or lightning, and guardian spirits; these might be considered polytheistic, since they lack one central deity. Many other tribes, however, believe in a Great Spirit or Creator Spirit who exists above the rest of the spirit world. This spirit may be impersonal, leading to Deism (explained in chapter 10), or personal and so more monotheistic in nature. Still others see this Great Spirit as a divine force in nature and, accordingly, are more pantheistic in outlook.

Another generally valid observation is that Native peoples highly value living in balance with the natural environment. While traditionally this was a physical necessity, it also found and continues today to find validity in their respect for the spirits they believe live in the natural realm. There have been exceptions on both sides, but among the most common sources of conflict between Native American and European American cultures has been disparity in how the land and nature are treated. As European settlement moved west across the continent, the cutting of forests, plowing of the soil, and decimation of buffalo herds and other game were viewed by Native peoples as a physical encroachment on their livelihood and an attack upon the spirits that were the providers of and even dwellers in those natural resources.

The focus of Native religions, even for believers in a Great Spirit or Creator, is not typically on that central deity (as in monotheistic religions), but rather on the surrounding spirit world that is believed to impact daily life. As with other animistic systems, maintaining good relations with the spirit realm is at the core of most beliefs and practices. Again, these religions are often described as practical, as they deal primarily with the pragmatic present.

Because the spirits are nearby and have certain demands or requirements in order to keep relationships with humans, it is possible to offend them, with negative consequences for individuals or even entire communities. Therefore, *taboos* are a common feature. In Western culture, this term is often used for actions prohibited on social, moral, or ethical grounds. In Native religions, taboos are behavioral requirements or prohibitions such that doing (or not doing) them would upset the balance of nature, bring negative magical power into individuals, or offend the spirits. Taboos are rigidly enforced, since failure to follow them may bring disastrous corporate consequences.

Native American religions rarely have priests or other full-time leaders. Everyone participates at some level. A few may have closer relationships with the spirit world and thus have ability or spiritual insight that benefits the community, most commonly in the form of healing. These medicine men (or women), as they were called by European observers, hold significant power but also great responsibility for the community's well-being.

The usual purpose of the many types of rituals and ceremonies is to draw the physical and spiritual worlds closer together. A familiar goal is that humans may obtain strength, endurance, or wisdom from one or more spirits. The best-known ritual for an individual is the Vision Quest, which, in some tribes, may be done by anyone needing special spiritual assistance, though they're most common for young men (occasionally young women) as part of entrance into adulthood. The quest typically involves isolation from the community and fasting for several days. The aim is to receive a vision of an animal (visually representing a particular spirit) that becomes the person's *totem*, believed then to guard and guide him or her throughout the rest of life.

The most common group ceremonies involve dancing and drumming, activities intended to help humans become more open to the spirit world. Dances may go on for hours or even days as the dancers disengage from the everyday world and seek communion with the spirits. Today, powwows are becoming increasingly common and nearly always include dancing. For some, this is more about recovering their culture than a religious exercise, but, again, Native peoples characteristically do not separate the sacred from the secular.

Beliefs regarding the afterlife are variable, but generally Native people do not fear dying. Most believe there is a place to which one's spirit goes at death. For some this is a happy place; for others it contains sadness. Usually people's spirits are considered to abide in this other plane of existence as long as they are remembered by those still living. As they are forgotten, their spirit gradually fades from existence.

An Extra Minute

NARs are seeing a resurgence of interest on the part of both Natives and non-Natives (usually those exploring New Age religions). Attendance at powwows has soared, and Natives knowledgeable about traditional practices arc in great demand. While some Natives are pleased that outsiders are interested, many others are concerned that more will be lost than gained. Some Native religious teachers have been known to alter symbols and practices slightly when teaching non-Natives.

African Traditional Religions

In terms of adherents, the largest animistic family is the African Traditional religions (ATRs). Africa contains fifty-plus countries and more than one thousand different people groups, each with its own religious variations on the animistic theme. Here, too, generalizations are possible, with exceptions.

ATRs have proven exceptionally resilient in the face of modernization. As Christianity and Islam spread across Africa, it was widely predicted that traditional religions would disappear by the end of the twentieth century. On the contrary, though a majority of today's Africans claim to be either Christian or Muslim, traditional religions are widely practiced. Both monotheistic religions face the problem of nominalism (from Latin, meaning "in name only"). Syncretism and parallelism are pervasive.

Syncretism is the blending of beliefs and practices from two different religions, and in most cases one of the two is animistic (e.g., the folk religions mentioned in chapter 8). Parallelism describes the practicing of two systems side by side without blending them. Think of the American churchgoer who regularly checks her horoscope, for instance, or the African Christian who attends church on Sunday but takes his sick child to the traditional healer.

Many Africans think of religion as something formal, and perhaps having a written scripture or holy books. They consider their animistic practices, passed down orally, simply to be cultural tradition. Often the formal religion (e.g., Christianity or Islam) is thought of as being for the "next life," while traditional practices help people through this one, filled with difficulties and calamities. Those are thought to be caused by various spirits, and ATRs are primarily concerned with making practical use of the spirit world's power.

Spirits may be recently deceased ancestors, nature-dwelling spirits (who inhabit forests, bodies of water, or the edges of cultivated fields), or other categories. Some folk Muslims have an additional category based on the Islamic belief in *jinn* (from which we get our English word *genie*), which are, according to the Qur'an, demonic spirits that serve Satan. All these spirit-types are believed to have influence over life events. ATRs use rituals, often carried out by specialists, to appease or influence spirits so that either they'll stop harming the petitioner (e.g., illness or calamity) or work on the petitioner's behalf to help achieve some goal (winning a game, passing an exam, or in some cases, bringing harm to an enemy).

Most African Traditional religions are deistic, maintaining belief in a creator god who is distant or disinterested in the people he made. It is the spirit world that must be dealt with, since it is close and active, and for those not influenced by Christianity or Islam, at death a person enters into this realm and remains near the places where he or she lived in the body.

Because of the way Africans view these ancestors, anthropologists refer to them as "the living dead." This refers not to anything like zombies or other such inventions, but rather to the perception of persons no longer physically living yet continuing to hover nearby as spirits. As with NARs, the dead are thought to continue in this state while remembered by those still alive, after which they fade from existence.

Illnesses are often attributed to an ancestral spirit in danger of being forgotten. When this is divined, a feast is held in memory of that person in order to bring healing to the sick one. This is why many Africans name their children after grandparents, aunts, and uncles. Anytime the child's name is called, the remembered namesake is less likely to be forgotten and bring calamity on them.

Rituals tend to consist of chants, songs, medicines (often herbal remedies that may benefit a sick person physically), and sacrifices. Typically the larger the request the bigger the sacrifice. While offerings of food, milk, or beer are common, many requests require a blood sacrifice. Usually this is a chicken or two; it could be a goat or, for community issues, a cow. Unlike the Christian or Jewish views, in ATRs, sacrifice is not an atonement or substitution for sin—it's a gift to the spirit being approached for help.

As to the variety of specialists who carry out ATR rituals, the common Western term *witch doctor* is inaccurate in most respects. Broadly speaking, these authorities can be categorized as either traditional healers or sorcerers, although both groups usually have sub-categories.

Traditional healers cure illnesses and help solve other life problems. A key endeavor for them is divination, wherein rituals are used to determine which spirit is causing a difficulty so that it can be appeased. They also produce fetishes, or charms, to be worn around the neck, wrist, waist, or ankle to ward off unwanted spirits. Sorcerers, though, are called upon to place curses and are generally feared, as their power is used only for evil purposes.

Spirits are tied to tribal locality, since they either are ancestors or inhabit local geographic features. Therefore, ATRs have no missionary outreach. They are viewed as specific to each tribe, so any one tribe sees no point in others sharing its convictions or following its rituals and practices.

An Extra Minute

Because of beliefs about ancestral spirits, burial location is critically important to traditional Africans. Silvanus Melea (S.M.) Otieno (1931–1986), a highly educated lawyer, was born into the Luo tribe near Lake Victoria in western Kenya. (Barack Obama's father also was a Luo.) Otieno married Wambui Waiyaki, a Kikuyu, and they lived most of their lives in Nairobi, largely disconnected from traditional life and its practices. After Otieno died, there was a five-month court case over his burial. He had left written instructions, verified by his wife, that he was to be buried on his farm outside Nairobi, but his Umira Kager clan of the Luo tribe insisted on ancestral land for the burial near Lake Victoria, some three hundred miles away. Millions of Kenyans followed the case as the local papers carried the daily proceedings verbatim. The courts eventually ruled for traditional law over statutory law; Otieno was buried on Umira Kager land, against his own (and his widow's) wishes.

Judaism: Historical Development

What makes a person Jewish? This seemingly basic question is not so easy to answer, even for Jewish people.

For most particular faiths described in this book, a person identifies either by birth—into a family belonging to that religion—or by adherence (even nominally) to its beliefs and practices. While that is true for some Jewish people, many who identify as Jewish practice no religion, or practice one other than Judaism. So for some, being Jewish is more about ethnicity or family traditions than religious beliefs. Generally, if one has a Jewish mother, one is considered Jewish. On the other hand, a few people who are not ethnically Jewish convert to Judaism through profession of belief in its teachings.

So what follows is primarily a description of the religion. Many who self-identify as Jewish do not hold these beliefs or follow these practices.

Judaism traces its origins to Abraham or, more properly, to his great-grandchildren: the Twelve Patriarchs, the sons of Jacob, whose name God changed to Israel. Genesis gives little detail about the religious practices of Abraham and his descendants. God established a covenant with him (see Genesis 12), and we read of his sincere faith and the offering of animal sacrifices, but it is not until hundreds of years later, when Moses receives the Law on Mount Sinai, that Judaism begins to take shape. The Exodus and the Mosaic Law are foundational to the establishment of Israel as a nation and Judaism as a religion in the formal sense.

Although the priests maintained the tabernacle and its services during and after Israel's conquest of Palestine, the biblical record in the books of Joshua and Judges indicates that not all the people actively practiced their faith. Many began to follow the religious practices of the surrounding nations, and this persisted in Israel for nearly a thousand years.

After the period of the monarchy began, and especially after the temple's construction by Solomon, most religious rituals took place in Jerusalem, and the Law's sacrificial system was centered in the temple. The subsequent division of the nation into two kingdoms (Northern/Israel and Southern/Judah) contributed to ongoing pluralism and syncretism. Religious observance by the masses grew or declined based on the current king's spiritual fervor. Godly kings, unfortunately, were few in Judah and virtually nonexistent in Israel.

Much of the Hebrew Scriptures (known to many as the Bible's Old Testament) describe this spiritual decline and the warning messages God sent through a number of prophets. Eventually, the predicted judgment came.

Israel was conquered initially by the Assyrians, and the people were taken into exile. In 586 BC, the Babylonians destroyed Jerusalem and its temple and took most of the surviving inhabitants into exile. This period was significant in the development of modern Judaism.

First, without the temple and the sacrificial system, new worship forms were developed, along with a theology to support them. Second, the people of Judah were now a minority in a foreign land; this, too, impacted theological thinking. Third, because the exiled people were from the land of Judah, they were first called Jews during this period. Last, although precise dates are unknown, the development of synagogues and rabbis began around this time.

After the Persians conquered the Babylonians, the Jewish exiles were allowed to return to Jerusalem and rebuild the temple, yet historians estimate only 10 percent went back to Palestine. As a colony, first of the Persians, then the Greeks, and finally the Romans, the Jewish people were generally free to practice their faith, but all three colonizing nations, especially the Greeks, exerted considerable influence on Jewish culture and religion. One result was a Greek-language translation of the Jewish Scriptures called the Septuagint.

Rome's destruction of Jerusalem and the second temple brought an end to national Israel, even in a colonized form, until the modern state was formed in AD 1948. It also brought major changes to Jewish religious practice. Scattered throughout Europe and Asia (called the *diaspora*), a decentralized Judaism developed around the synagogue and the rabbi. With no new revealed Scripture for nearly five hundred years, no temple, no priesthood, and no sacrificial system, the rabbis began to think, debate, and write about how to keep the Law in the face of these new realities.

These writings, called the *Mishnah*, were compiled around AD 200, though much of their content had existed as oral tradition for several centuries. Further rabbinic writings, more applicational in nature (in general terms answering the *how* rather than *what* of the Mishnah), were compiled over the next several hundred years to become the *Gemarah*. Their combination is called the Talmud, which has both Palestinian and Babylonian versions and is the primary basis of modern Judaism (see chapter 12).

One last factor that has shaped Jewish life and theology over the past two millennia is persecution. The Roman emperors, the pogroms of medieval Europe, the czars and Stalin in Russia, the holocaust of Hitler's Germany—these only represent the best-known examples of anti-Semitism. The Jewish people have faced it all, from job discrimination to outright genocide. It's amazing that given the current Arab-Israeli conflict, for many centuries Jewish people usually found more welcome in Muslim lands than in Christian Europe. All of this has shaped modern Judaism's beliefs and practices, and anti-Semitism is still a chief concern for Jewish people today.

An Extra Minute

In the gospel accounts, Jesus often comes into verbal conflict with the scribes and the Pharisees. These groups attempted to strictly follow the Law but differed with Jesus (and often with each other) over correct interpretation and application. They also tended toward legalism and put the finer points of behavior above the attitude of the heart. Many of the oral traditions they followed ultimately were written down, and these scholarly opinions found their way into the Mishnah.

Judaism: Today

I t is impossible to understand modern Judaism without knowing the events and experiences of the Jewish people since the time of Moses (briefly outlined in chapter 11). In its number of followers, Judaism is among the smallest of the world's living religions, with slightly more than fourteen million adherents globally, yet it exerts a proportionally larger influence on world affairs today, in part because of the modern state of Israel, formed in 1948.

Many people, particularly Christians familiar with the Old Testament—the Hebrew Scriptures—think of Judaism in terms of what they've read in Exodus or Deuteronomy. Therefore, we must note that modern Judaism is Rabbinic, or Talmudic. Without a temple or sacrificial system, much of the Law cannot be followed. Over many centuries, influential rabbis have reflected and written on how to practice the Jewish faith under changed circumstances. The Talmud (see chapter 11) is the collection of those reflections and the basis for modern Judaism.

Jewish life today is primarily lived out in the home and secondarily in the synagogue. Practicing Judaism is more about daily life than about specified beliefs or formal rituals, although these do exist. *Shabat*, the Sabbath, begins at home on Friday at sundown; many who observe it faithfully do not attend synagogue regularly. Kosher dietary laws, an elaborate system of what can be eaten, when it can be eaten, and how to prepare it, were expanded by the rabbis from biblical commands to avoid the meat of certain animals and, in particular, Exodus 34:26, which states, "You shall not boil a young goat in its mother's milk." From this came a complete separation of meat and dairy products, and the dishes used to cook and serve them, in a kosher kitchen.

Nearly pandemic persecution, in particular the Holocaust, has had profound influence on modern Jewish thinking and theology. Most notable is the rise of Zionism, a movement that began in the nineteenth century to support the creation of a state where Jewish people could live without fear of persecution by their own government. The Zionist movement today supports the defense and development, politically and militarily, of Israel. Not all Jewish people have Zionist leanings.

Theological differences have resulted in multiple branches of Judaism today. The largest group worldwide, including in Israel—while not an organized branch—is non-observant Jews, who do not follow Jewish religious practices at all. The largest official segment is the Orthodox branch, which strives to keep all 613 *mitzvot* (commandments) of the Mosaic law. Some ultra-Orthodox (or Hasidic) subgroups, usually following the teachings of a particular rabbi, are even stricter than the Orthodox. Some of these have missionary organizations that target, primarily, the less strict and non-observant Jews.

By contrast, the Reform movement, popular mostly in Europe and the U.S., has sought to understand and practice Judaism in more modern ways. Christians would understand this branch of Judaism as more theologically liberal. For example, while most Orthodox Jews still anticipate a personal Messiah and believe in a future resurrection of the dead, Reform Jews await a messianic age of peace that will be brought about by human effort, and they have no expectations of life after physical death.

Between the Orthodox and Reform branches is Conservative Judaism, found mostly in the U.S. Believing Judaism must adapt to today's world, but finding Reform departures from Talmudic customs excessive, Conservative Jews seek to keep the 613 *mitzvot*, but with twenty-first-century interpretations. For example, Orthodox Jews will not drive on the Sabbath and must live near enough to a synagogue to walk to Shabat services; Conservative Jews do not believe driving is a prohibited Sabbath activity. Reconstructionist Judaism grew out of the Conservative movement and focuses on the importance of culture as well as religion in understanding what it means to be Jewish.

Perhaps the most important life event for a Jewish person is becoming an adult, marked by the ceremony of Bar Mitzvah for boys and, in Reform and Conservative Judaism, Bat Mitzvah for girls (at ages thirteen and twelve, respectively). The term means "son/daughter of the commandments." At this point, theologically, a Jewish person is now morally responsible to keep the Law. When the rich young ruler tells Jesus he has kept the commandments "from my youth" (Luke 18:21), he could have said, "since my Bar Mitzvah." Traditionally, this important rite of passage is marked with much celebration by the extended family in addition to special synagogue services. In small Jewish communities, this is significant because a minimum of ten adult males are necessary to form a congregation.

The head of each synagogue is a rabbi. Reform Judaism encourages female rabbis; Orthodox rabbis must be men; Conservative Judaism leaves to each congregation whether or not they will accept a female rabbi. The person who actually leads synagogue services, however, is the cantor, or *hazzan*. Large congregations seek a cantor who not only sings well but also can compose original music. Usually the cantor is also responsible for coaching young people in Hebrew as they prepare for their Bar or Bat Mitzvah.

Misunderstood by both Jews and Christians is Messianic Judaism. Messianic Jews are ethnically Jewish but believe Jesus of Nazareth is the Messiah promised to the Jewish people. Following centuries of persecution and anti-Semitism by Christians, Jewish people no longer accept Messianic Jews as Jewish, believing them to have become Gentiles. And because many Messianic Jews gather in their own congregations and retain Jewish cultural forms of worship, neither do some Christians accept them. They are best seen as ethnically and culturally Jewish and theologically Christian (in accepting the New Testament). There are about four hundred Messianic congregations in the U.S.

An Extra Minute

Ethnic stereotypes tend to exaggerate or distort observations about a particular group. Today's athletic success by African-Americans is attributed by some to a biological advantage in muscle structure (despite scientific evidence proving no genetic difference). In the 1920s and 1930s, Jewish people were widely believed to have an inherited racial advantage in playing basketball, and many of the early professional teams had a high proportion of Jewish players.

Zoroastrianism

How many people do you know who believe that after they die God will weigh their deeds and, as long as they have at least 50 percent good deeds, will allow them into heaven? This idea of God using balance scales to weigh deeds is held by many, including quite a number who call themselves Christians. But this concept is definitely not found in the Bible. So where did it come from?

Zoroastrianism, a religion most people have never heard of, was the first to put forth the concept of judgment by weighing good and bad deeds, called ethical dualism. Due to their geographic distribution today, and because persecution in some countries forces them to keep a low profile, it is difficult to know how many Zoroastrians there are. Estimates range from a low of 150,000 to as many as several million worldwide. The most reliable figures place the number at 250,000.

The nomenclature comes from the Latinization of its founder's name. Zoroaster was from Persia (present-day Iran), so today he usually is referred to by his Persian name, Zarathustra. In 1300 BC, when he likely lived (life dates vary from 1400–1000 BC), Persia was polytheistic, and Zarathustra was a priest (in fact, he's the only founder of a world religion who ever served as one). He had many religious questions, and according to the *Gathas* (a portion of the sacred Zoroastrian book *Avesta*), in the midst of his seeking he had a vision of an angel who told him there was only one true god, named *Ahura Mazda*, and Zarathustra was to be his prophet. Over the next ten years, further visions revealed to him the basis of the religion that came to bear his name.

Zarathustra preached this new message for over a decade before winning his first convert. Even by the time of his death there were very few followers. His disciples, however, persevered in spreading the message of Ahura Mazda, and by 500 BC it was the dominant religion of the Persian Empire (adherents included Kings Cyrus [Daniel 10]) and Ahasuerus (or Xerxes [Esther]). Even in Jesus' day it was still the majority religion in western and central Asia.

One universal human problem all religions seek to handle is the presence of both good and evil in the world. *Dualism* is the philosophical term for this perpetual struggle, and religions wrestle with it in many ways. Monotheistic faiths (Judaism, Christianity, and Islam) teach that God is good but is opposed by Satan. Satan, however, is not God's equal, for Satan is a created being. Thus these religions are not actually dualistic; if they taught two separate and equal supreme powers they would no longer be monotheistic.

Zarathustra developed a true dualistic monotheism. He taught that two spirits emanate from the one God: *Spenta Mainyu*, the Beneficent Spirit, and *Angra Mainyu*, the Evil Spirit. They are equal in power and have always coexisted, so Zoroastrianism is both dualistic and monotheistic.

Spenta Mainyu created the world to enlist humans in his effort to defeat evil. How does he ensure that humans help the good side? By establishing moral guidelines and a day of judgment, where deeds are weighed. Heaven awaits the good; hell, the evil.

Zarathustra's descriptions of hell, graphic and terrifying, are the basis of many people's assumptions about what hell is like (even if they don't realize the source). It's intriguing that the Bible tells just enough about hell that we know we don't want to go there, but forgoes vivid details as found in the *Avesta*.

Zoroastrianism prevailed in central Asia and the eastern Mediterranean world for about a thousand years, but after the Muslim armies from Arabia conquered Persia in the seventh century AD, persecution of Zoroastrians followed. Eventually most migrated to India, where they became known as *Parsees* (from the Hindi word for Persians). The majority today still lives in India, where they're considered a caste (social class) despite the significant differences in religious belief from Hinduism. Because of their high moral code, they are honest and highly successful businesspeople, owning some of the largest corporations in India. Some Zoroastrians still live in Iran (modern-day Persia).

In Zarathustra's view, air, water, earth, and fire are pure elements; it is immoral to pollute them. Zoroastrian worship consists primarily of prayers, both individual and corporate. There are also ceremonies for significant life events (rites of passage), such as becoming an adult, marriage, and others. Temples maintain a sacred flame around which most ceremonies take place.

Although the religion originally spread through conversion by itinerant preachers, Zoroastrianism today is not a missionary religion. Indeed, many Zoroastrians believe conversion is impossible, that one must be born into the religion. Conversions do happen, however, and some communities have been more accepting of converts than others.

An Extra Minute

Because Zoroastrians are declining in number, survival of the religion is a significant issue to them. They are using the Internet to create virtual communities and even online worship centers to keep the community together. Many losses from the faith are due to young Zoroastrians marrying followers of other religions, so online matchmaking services are a popular effort to help geographically scattered Zoroastrians find marriage partners within the religion. The designer of one of the larger websites is a Minnesota-born convert from Roman Catholicism.

Islam: Beginnings

Islam is the world's second largest religion, with about 1.6 billion followers in 2010 (more than 20 percent of the earth's population). Including biological growth, it is also the globe's fastest-growing, and is the majority religion in forty-nine countries. Contemporary politics and the issue of terrorism have thrust Islam into the worldwide spotlight as never before.

Islam is an Arabic word meaning "submission," and the religion's central theme is submission to the will of God. So a Muslim is one who submits to God's will, which is revealed in the Qur'an, the Islamic holy book (*Qur'an*, an Arabic word meaning "recite," is often transliterated *Koran* in English texts). Although the Arabic language and culture are central to Islam, only 25 percent of the world's Muslims are ethnically Arab, and the four countries with the largest Muslim populations (Indonesia, Pakistan, Bangladesh, and India) are all outside the Middle East.

Some older books on history and religion refer to this faith as Mohammedanism. This is inaccurate and offensive to Muslims, as they do not worship Muhammad. Although they revere him greatly and follow his example in many ways, they insist he was just a man. To deify him, they say, is contrary to Muhammad's own teaching.

Islam teaches that God has sent a long line of prophets to reveal his will to humans, and many Muslims would say Islam has existed since Adam's creation. However, to understand Islam today, we need to look at sixth-century Arabia and a man named Muhammad, considered Islam's final and greatest prophet (in Muslim writings, his or any prophet's name usually is followed by *pbuh*, meaning, "peace be upon him"; variations in English spellings of *Muhammad* are attempts to approximate the sounds of the Arabic letters).

Muhammad was born about AD 570, in Mecca, both a trade center and pilgrimage site even before Islam. As a young man, he frequently went outside the city to meditate in nearby caves. On one occasion, a powerful supernatural being appeared and told Muhammad to recite the message he was given.

Frightened and in shock, Muhammad related this event to his relatives and close friends. He initially believed the supernatural being was Satan, but his friends convinced him otherwise and encouraged him to return to the cave. This being, claiming to be the angel Gabriel, appeared to Muhammad many times over a period of several years, each time giving him more of the message that eventually developed into the Qur'an.

Many parts of the Qur'an bear striking resemblance to portions of the sacred texts of Zoroastrianism, Judaism, and Christianity. Because Mecca was a center for trade, people of many faiths passed through it; Muhammad, engaged in managing camel caravans, undoubtedly encountered some of these. In addition, a sizeable number of Jewish communities were in Arabia at the time. But Muslims insist this had no influence on Muhammad and that the Qur'an was dictated to him directly—any similarities are because the other religions are like Islam rather than the other way around. Further, Muhammad was illiterate, so while he may have talked with followers of monotheistic religions, he did not read from any of their scriptures.

The religion of pre-Islamic Arabia was polytheistic and idol-worshiping. By contrast, the message given to Muhammad was that there is only one God, who could not be represented by any image. While some believed his reports, most citizens of Mecca resented and opposed his message. Persecution and threats against his life increased until, in 622, he and his followers escaped and went 250 miles north to the city of Yathrib (later renamed Medina). Muslims call this event the *Hijra* (migration, or escape), and rather than Muhammad's birth, this event marks the first year of the Muslim calendar.

In Medina, Muhammad organized his growing number of followers and continued to teach. By 630, the Muslims had become powerful enough to conquer Mecca, destroy the idols at the center of the Meccan religion, and establish Islam as the Arabian Peninsula's primary religion. Muhammad died shortly afterward (632), yet his followers quickly spread the faith westward. Even though this often coincided with military conquests by Arab armies, forced conversions were not the norm, at least among Jews and Christians, whom Islam considers people of the Book.

Political and spiritual factors in the Byzantine Empire also contributed to Islam's rapid conversion rate among the conquered, non-Arab peoples of western Asia and North Africa. After conquering Spain, the Muslim advance was decisively halted at the Battle of Tours (732), in southern France, though it was many years before Muslims were expelled from Spain and Portugal.

To the east, Islam spread into central Asia, northern India, East Africa, and eventually to present-day Indonesia. While military conquest was a factor, as it was in the West, trade was also a significant means by which the message was propagated. In northern India, the Muslims ruled but did not convert the Hindu majority. In East Africa, where Arab settlements had existed since pre-Islamic times and the trade included slaves, little effort was made at converting the local people, since enslaving fellow Muslims was generally forbidden. This changed early in the 1800s, when Great Britain outlawed the slave trade throughout its empire and British naval vessels began to seize Arab slave ships in the Indian Ocean.

After nearly two centuries of incredibly rapid expansion, the spread of Islam slowed until the twentieth century. In the post-colonial era, it again began spreading. Globalization and migration have made a truly worldwide religion of Islam. Like Christianity, it believes it is a universal faith all people should accept, and it has organizations that seek to propagate it in new places. Today, there is probably no nation in the world without the presence of Islam.

An Extra Minute

Islamic beliefs and practices are based on the Qur'an, the *Sunna*, and the *Hadith*. The Qur'an is held to be sacred scripture, dictated to Muhammad by Gabriel. Many questions about faith and practice arose after Muhammad's death, so Muslims asked those who had known the prophet and were still alive what he said or did in various situations. These were eventually written down and collected into the Sunna (or Sunnah) meaning "Traditions." This multi-volume collection is sometimes referred to as the Hadith (Sayings), as it includes what Muhammad said. Although not considered a holy book like the Qur'an, in daily life, the Sunna is used more frequently.

Islam: Foundations

Essential to the religion of Islam are the Five Pillars, or obligations, that are required of all Muslims. These are, in English:

1. Reciting the Creed
2. Praying five times daily
3. Almsgiving
4. Fasting
5. Making the pilgrimage to Mecca

Let's look at each in more detail:

1. The Creed (*Shahada*) is "There is no God but God and Muhammad is the prophet of God." These are the first words heard by a baby born into a Muslim family, the last words heard on the Muslim deathbed, and words heard every day of life in between. The Creed is repeated as part of the daily prayers (below), and many Muslims repeat the Creed before opening the Qur'an to read. The Creed is written in Arabic, and usually the

local language, as well, on every mosque in the world. A person converts to Islam by reciting the Creed in front of witnesses.

The first phrase denotes the oneness of God and is similar to the Hebrew *Shema* (Deuteronomy 6:4). The second part, uniquely Muslim, establishes Muhammad as God's messenger or prophet. Because the Creed is often translated into English as "There is no God but Allah . . ." non-Muslims frequently and mistakenly believe it to mean that *Allah* is the proper name for the God of Islam. *Allah*, however, is the generic Arabic word for God and is used in the Arabic translation of the Bible as well.

2. Prayers (*salat*) are to be offered five times daily. Sunrise and sunset determine the timing, so Muslims in different parts of the world pray at different times. The first prayer is just before sunrise, the second at midday, the third late afternoon, the fourth just after sunset, and the fifth about two hours after sunset (full nightfall). Before praying, a Muslim must wash his face (also rinsing the mouth, nose, and ears), hands, arms (up to the elbows), feet, and ankles. The prayers are memorized Arabic phrases, primarily from the Qur'an, repeated with accompanying movements, including bowing, kneeling, and prostrating oneself.

3. Almsgiving (*zakat*) is the required giving of 2.5 percent of one's wealth. In that respect it is more like a tax than a freewill offering, although it may not be rigidly enforced outside Islamic countries. The contributions are to help the poor and to support Muslim institutions, such as the mosque and Qur'anic schools. Zakat may be given directly to a poor person, collected at the mosque, or placed in a box at many Muslim-run businesses.

4. Fasting (*sawm*) is required from sunrise to sunset for thirty days during the month of Ramadan, the ninth month of the Muslim calendar, the month when Muhammad is said to have experienced his first revelation. Because Muslims follow a lunar calendar, the date of Islamic holidays is different each year according to the commonly used Gregorian calendar.

During daytime hours, Muslims are to abstain from all food, drink, smoking, and sexual relations. When Ramadan falls during the hot season in tropical countries, an entire day without water or other fluids can be arduous, and the fast requires considerable discipline. According to Muslim tradition, the fast begins when there's enough light to distinguish a black thread from a white one and ends when the opposite is true.

Even young children may practice for a day or two, and by the time a Muslim reaches mid-teens, they are expected to keep the full fast. Besides young children, pregnant or nursing women, the sick, and travelers are exempt from the fast, though many Muslims believe they must later make up those days. The end of the month of fasting is celebrated with a major holiday called Eid-al-Fitr. Family gatherings, feasting, visiting friends, and gift-giving are all part of this happy celebration. After the Eid holiday, a few pious Muslims fast an additional ten days, seeking more favor with God.

Some Muslims follow the calendar to determine when the fasting month begins and ends. Others depend on the actual sighting of the new moon. If the sky is cloudy, Muslims may listen intently to the radio to hear if others nearby with clearer weather have seen the new moon. Going by the moon, there is always the possibility of a twenty-nine-day (rather than thirty-day) fast.

5. Pilgrimage (*Hajj*) to Mecca at least once in a lifetime is required of all Muslims who have sufficient health and financial means. Mecca was already a pilgrimage site in pre-Islamic times; the Meccans' refusal to let Muhammad and his followers make a pilgrimage from Medina was one of the factors leading up to the Battle of Hunayn, in 630.

The Hajj takes place during the twelfth and last month of the Muslim calendar. Ten days are needed to complete the required acts, and throughout the time in Mecca all Muslims are clothed in simple white garments so there is no distinguishing rich from poor. Some poor but pious Muslims will save money their entire lives to make the pilgrimage. Today, with hundreds of thousands going each year, there are challenging logistics for the Saudi government, which deftly arranges for housing and feeding all these people. After the Hajj, a Muslim is given the title *haji*, and some believe all their sins are forgiven after completing the pilgrimage.

An Extra Minute

Fast, or feast?

Because the fast during Ramadan is kept during daylight hours only, Muslims do eat during the night. In many homes the daily schedule changes to accommodate nighttime meals. For those who can afford it, special foods are common at Ramadan meals. For the typical family, the food bill is more than double the norm during this month; some non-Muslims are disdainful of this approach to fasting. Nonetheless, it takes no small restraint to abstain from all food and drink for so many hours, especially in hot seasons with long days, and thirty straight at that.

Islam: Beliefs

In addition to the Five Pillars (see chapter 15), Muslims are obliged to hold other beliefs. First among these is that, unlike Judaism, wherein a person can be an atheist and still be considered Jewish, a Muslim must believe in God.

For other monotheistic faiths, and especially Judaism and Christianity, a common question is whether Muslims worship the same God. For American Christians, the frequent question "Is Allah God?" creates confusion. Because Islam is so closely tied to Arabic language and culture, many people think *Allah* is a special Muslim name for God or refers specifically to the God of Islam. Again, however, *Allah* is the generic Arabic word for God (like the Greek *Theos*, Spanish *Dios*, or Hebrew *Elohim*) and also is used in the Arabic Bible (there are millions of Arabic-speaking Christians in Lebanon, Syria, Palestine, Jordan, Egypt, Iraq, and elsewhere). The wording of the question likewise assumes that the English word *God* refers exclusively to the God of the Bible, but English-speaking followers of any religion use that word to refer to their deity.

So the question should be "Is the God revealed in the Qur'an the same God revealed in the Bible?" Muslims believe they worship the God of Abraham, and thus, the same God as Jews and Christians. While there is a real historical connection, along with some similarities in beliefs about God's attributes, there are many significant theological differences as to God's nature and relationship to humans. In the Bible, God reveals himself to Moses as *YHWH*; in Islam, God's name is unknown. Muslims refer to the ninety-nine names of God, but the actual or correct name is a mystery.

Muslims sometimes finger a string of beads resembling a rosary. The thirty-three beads in the usual string are utilized as a memory device for reciting the ninety-nine names, since it is believed that prayers offered to God using the correct name will be heard. Key attributes revealed in the Bible that differ from the Qur'an include God's triune nature (Father, Son, and Spirit), his love for humankind, and his provision of salvation by grace.

Some Muslim and Christian beliefs are very similar but not identical. Both believe angels are created, supernatural beings that serve God. However, where Christians believe Satan and the demonic realm are angels who have rebelled against God, Muslims believe they are a different type of spiritual being, created from fire. Both believe God sent prophets with messages for humankind. Some prophets named in the Qur'an are also found in the Bible, including Adam, Noah, Abraham, Moses, David, Solomon, John the Baptist, and Jesus, but according to the biblical record, not all in that group held the role of prophet. Muslims also are taught that the prophets lived near-perfect lives, free from at least any major sin, and were protected from all harm. The Bible is frank in revealing the prophets' human failings and records that many were persecuted and even killed for their faithfulness in proclaiming God's message.

Muslims believe that some prophets were given books; the books named are the Torah (Pentateuch) of Moses, the Zabur (Psalms) of David, the Injil (gospel) of Jesus, and the Qur'an (Recitation) of Muhammad. The Qur'an claims that the messages of all these books are the same. Since Muhammad was nonliterate, and books were rare prior to the printing press, he never read the Bible and genuinely believed this was true. When the differences were discovered some time after his death, the Muslim explanation was that the Jews and Christians had changed their books, which now are "corrupted." While this might have seemed plausible in the eighth century, Muslims still are taught that the Bible we have today is a corrupted book, even though modern textual research and the hundreds of discovered ancient manuscripts prove there were no such changes.

Another core belief for Muslims is the Day of Judgment, when the dead will be raised, stand before God, and be sent either to heaven or hell. While it is hoped that one's good deeds and submission to God will earn his favor, there is no way to know in advance the outcome. Traditionally this decision was considered permanent, but a more recent teaching is that everyone will go to hell first, to be punished for their sins, and then go to heaven. Some believe this applies to everyone, while others are taught that only Muslims eventually will go to heaven. Muslims acknowledge that Muhammad died and awaits the Judgment Day. Early writings indicate that Jesus, whom Muslims believe was taken into heaven without dying, will return to raise the dead on Judgment Day. More recently, the teaching has been altered to say that Jesus will raise Muhammad and then turn the task over to him to finish.

Most controversial among Muslim beliefs is *Jihad* (an Arabic word meaning "struggle"). The translation "holy war," somewhat misleading, is disliked by most Muslims. The Qur'an clearly limits Jihad to defending Islam and Muslims against attack. For moderate Muslims, this means struggling to live a life that's a good testimony for Islam. For fundamentalists, the defense includes physical war as well. From their perspective, the recent wars in Afghanistan and Iraq are invasions of Muslim lands by nonbelievers, so they are obligated to help defend their fellow Muslims. Extremists even try to legitimize terrorism as a defense against Western (i.e., non-Muslim) cultural, economic, and political encroachment.

For Muslims, everything in life is either *haram* (forbidden) or *halal* (permitted). The forbidden includes eating pork, drinking alcohol, using drugs, gambling, and adultery. It is generally accepted that an action is permitted if not specifically forbidden; specifically permitted are men marrying up to four wives (if they are treated equally) and divorce. *Halal* also refers to the proper slaughtering of animals and the preparation of meat. The procedure is similar to kosher preparation and, in fact, Muslims can eat kosher meat. Jews, however, will not eat halal meat.

An Extra Minute

Many of the hot-dog carts in Manhattan's financial district are run by Muslims from the Middle East or North Africa. The hot dogs they sell are kosher rather than halal, so anyone, Christian, Jew, Muslim, or otherwise, can enjoy lunch with a clear conscience.

Islam: Theology

Monotheistic Islam shares many similarities with Judaism and Christianity, along with Zoroastrianism and Baha'i. But there are important differences. For example, Muslims share Judaism's belief in God's absolute oneness. Christians also believe God is one Being and that he eternally exists as three persons. The Qur'an and the Bible likewise agree on many of God's attributes, but again there are areas of disagreement. That the same or similar words are sometimes used with different meanings generates misunderstanding. For instance, Muslims and Christians both say God is merciful, but the Bible adds to this his grace and love. Minus these attributes, salvation as a divine gift is incomprehensible to Muslims.

All the monotheistic religions believe their scriptures to be a revelation from God. Muslims believe the revealing takes place by a process of dictation. The Qur'an, they say, exists eternally in heaven, and Gabriel came to earth and dictated the book to God's messenger Muhammad. Christians believe in a process called *inspiration*, from a Greek word meaning "God-breathed."

The Holy Spirit inspired the Bible's human authors so that God's message is communicated while retaining the writers' individual styles and vocabulary.

These views have significant impact on thoughts about translation. The Bible was rendered into Syriac and Latin within a century of the New Testament's completion. Other translations followed; the combination of the printing press and the Protestant Reformation unleashed a tidal wave of translations into other languages. In contrast, the "true message" of the Qur'an can be read only in Arabic. Though translations exist, they're considered paraphrases, not authoritative. The many Muslims who don't read Arabic often use editions with parallel columns in Arabic and their own language.

Beliefs also vary as to the nature of humanity. While Christians believe everyone is born with a sin nature inherited from Adam and Eve, Muslims believe each person is born a clean slate and can choose to do either good or evil. The biblical creation account says humans were created in the image of God and given a mandate to be stewards of creation. For example, God brought all the animals to Adam, and whatever he called them became their name (Genesis 2:19–20). According to the Qur'an's account, God told Adam what the animal's names were, and Adam memorized them.

Regarding salvation, the Bible teaches that God has graciously provided salvation as a free gift to those who trust the righteousness of Jesus. No human effort can pay sin's penalty. Assurance of salvation is based on God's promises, because it is his work. The Qur'an teaches that whether someone goes to heaven or hell is ultimately up to God's will. By submitting to his will during this earthly life, one can hope to earn God's favor and will find out on Judgment Day whether or not it has been granted.

Perhaps most interesting, from a Christian viewpoint, are Muslim beliefs about Jesus. Islam acknowledges him as a great prophet, second only to Muhammad. But even Muslims are often unaware of all the Qur'an teaches about Jesus. First, it affirms his miraculous birth to the Virgin Mary. As is common in the Middle East to this day, the Qur'an refers to people by their first name and their father's name, using the Arabic word *ibn*. Jesus is the only person in the Qur'an identified by his mother's name. Second, he is given the title *Masih*, the Arabic equivalent of the English *Messiah*. The Arabic way of pronouncing his name is *Isa*, so in the Qur'an he is called "Isa Masih ibn Mariamu," Jesus the Messiah, the son of Mary.

Jesus is also described as a miracle-worker and is the only person the Qur'an mentions as living a sinless life. In the past century, as there has been more interaction between Christianity and Islam, Muslims are being taught that Muhammad also lived sinlessly. His confession of sin and uncertainty about the Day of Judgment in the Qur'an and Sunna, it is said, are examples for his followers. Further, it is now claimed that Muhammad also worked a miracle, being nonliterate yet producing the Qur'an, considered a masterpiece of Arabic literature.

The Qur'an teaches that Jesus ascended into heaven and is coming again at the resurrection day. With the Bible and the Qur'an both affirming so many aspects of his life, why are there two religions? Because the Qur'an also denies key biblical statements about Jesus. Muslims agree Jesus' conception was the work of God's Spirit in a virgin, but they disagree that this makes him anything other than an ordinary human. Islam denies his incarnation and deity and considers the term *Son of God* blasphemous.

Further, they understand the Qur'an to teach that Jesus did not die on a cross. God, they say, would never allow such a terrible thing to happen to one of his holy prophets. Without Jesus' death, there is, of course, no atonement for sin and no salvation. In fact, Islam denies even the possibility of one person being able to bear punishment for the sin of others.

This brief comparison shows the core beliefs of Islam and Christianity to be substantially different. This isn't surprising, since, as noted in chapter 1, all religions are not the same, and the similarities are usually only on the surface.

An Extra Minute

The English text of the Qur'an, without footnotes, is approximately two-thirds the length of the New Testament.

18

Islam: Varieties and Issues

Even small religions show amazing variety within their beliefs and practices, so it's no surprise that Islam is not monolithic.

First, as with any religion, there are differing levels of commitment and participation. At one end of the spectrum among professing Muslims are the nominal (non-practicing). Next are the Conformists, whose personal attitude is indifference or even unbelief but who follow the rituals due to family or societal pressure. While this might seem primarily limited to Muslim-majority countries where *Sharia* (Islamic law) is enforced, even where there's legal religious freedom, families and communities can exert tremendous pressure.

Next, the Reformers are not an official branch (as in Judaism); the term refers to Muslims who sincerely believe Islam is the true religion but that the Qur'an must be understood and applied in the present, separating it from its seventh-century cultural roots. The Moderates, probably the largest group worldwide, are sincere in their belief, appreciate Islam's positive aspects (family, community, morality, etc.), and reject more radical interpretations.

And even the Fundamentalists, at the far end of the spectrum, have subgroups. All agree on a literal, almost rigid interpretation of the Qur'an, but some (e.g., the Taliban) teach law practices that go beyond the Qur'an. Some Fundamentalists actively propagate their faith and believe Islam's message will eventually reach and persuade everyone, yet they renounce violence. The most extreme Fundamentalists—the ones recruiting suicide bombers and planning acts of terror—believe Western cultural, political, and economic encroachment must be stopped by any and all means. (The above categories are adapted and expanded from a conversation with Samer Abdulraman.)

In addition, Islam has divided into groups like denominations (in Christian terms). By far the largest, including more than 80 percent of the world's Muslims, are the Sunnis. Followers of the Qur'an and the Traditions (Sunna), they have little hierarchical structure. An *imam* (prayer leader of a mosque) leads prayers and usually preaches a Friday sermon but has no formal authority outside the mosque he serves. Scholars and writers seek to influence fellow Muslims to their interpretations but cannot command obedience.

As Islam grew and expanded geographically, differing interpretations and even different editions of the Sunna emerged and were refined. These eventually coalesced into four schools of thought: the Hanifites, Malikites, Shafi'ites, and Hanbalites, each based on the teachings of one eighth- or ninth-century founding scholar. Each is strongest in a particular geographic area, although contemporary migration patterns have resulted in some mixing.

In the U.S., it's common for Muslims from all these schools to pray in the same mosque. Each has millions of followers, and there is much variation of belief even within each group.

Generally, though, the Shafi'ites, found primarily in East Africa and South and Southeast Asia, are most willing to adapt Islamic teaching to local cultural norms. The Hanbalites, found in Saudi Arabia (Islam's center), are the most conservative.

Followers of the Wahabi movement, which began in eighteenth-century Arabia, are strict traditionalists who resist all change. Due to the oil wealth in Saudi Arabia, the Wahabis finance a global missionary movement to spread their message.

The other main branch is made of the Shi'ites. The Sunni/Shi'ite division occurred early on in Islam, initially over the question of leadership after Muhammad's death. He left no succession plan, and opinions varied on how to choose a *caliph* (leader). Those future Sunnis said the caliph should be chosen by consensus based on qualifications (early on, the highest qualification was close association with Muhammad during his lifetime). Those who became the Shi'ites believed the caliphate should be hereditary and that Muhammad had named his cousin and son-in-law, Ali, as his successor.

After three non-family caliphs, Ali was appointed. But in a period of confusion and power struggles he never fully gained control over the Muslim world and was murdered after barely five years. The Umayyad dynasty seized leadership and civil war followed. At the Battle of Karbala, in present-day Iraq, Ali's son Husayn was killed. The Shi'ites now consider him to be a martyr and his death is commemorated each year. Shi'ites have subdivided into many groups (e.g., Ismaili, Bohra, Ithna asheri), following different imams or traditions.

Over the centuries, the two branches have developed some doctrinal differences as well. Shi'ite imams are thought to be divinely appointed, and they speak with God's authority (somewhat like the Roman Catholic pope). Shi'ites also await the Mahdi, a future messianic figure, who will come to put everything right on the earth. In most parts of the world, Sunnis and

Shi'ites live together in harmony, but disputes do occur. From 1980–1988, Shi'ite Iran and Sunni-ruled Iraq fought a bitter and bloody war. Of the multiple factors in the conflict (not all of them religious), one was access to the many Shi'ite pilgrimage sites in Iraq, most notably Karbala, where Husayn was martyred. Attacks by one group on the other occur with some frequency in Iraq, Pakistan, Afghanistan, and elsewhere.

A small but interesting group is the Ahmadiyyas, who began in the late nineteenth century and see themselves as a revival movement, restoring proper Islamic practice. They follow Mirza Ghulam Ahmad, who claimed to be the long-awaited Mahdi of peace and justice; other Muslims reject this claim, and most view them as a cult or heretical sect (somewhat like the Christian view of Jehovah's Witnesses). Their unique theology includes views regarding Jesus' death and return. They believe he was put on the cross but passed out instead of dying. After recovering, Jesus went to the Kashmir region of India, where later he died a normal death and was buried. The Ahmadiyyas are very active in missionary work, both among other Muslims and non-Muslims.

Sufis are mystics, seeking more personal connection with God through ascetic practice and renouncing the material world for divine communion. They are not another branch, but rather a movement within Islam that crosses all lines of Sunni and Shi'ite. Sometimes suspect by other Muslims, sufis have at times faced persecution for their practices.

An Extra Minute

Whirling Dervishes are an extreme, centuries-old, fraternal form of Sufism. They twirl in one spot for hours, hoping to achieve an ecstatic state where they can more closely experience God.

The Nation of Islam

The Nation of Islam is probably best known for the Million Man March, held on the National Mall in Washington, DC, October 16, 1995. Louis Farrakhan, its leader, gave the keynote address and led the huge crowd in pledges to "take responsibility for their lives and families, and commit to stopping the scourges of drugs, violence, and unemployment." Social and economic improvement for African-Americans through self-discipline and moral living has always been part of the Nation's beliefs, and it has made a positive contribution to the lives of many in this regard.

The Nation of Islam began in 1930. In this period of Jim Crow laws, legal segregation, and horrendous discrimination, millions of poor, rural African-Americans from southern states migrated to northern cities in search of work. Conditions often were no better than what they'd left behind. Into this situation a man named Wallace D. Fard appeared, in Detroit, preaching a message of Black supremacy. He said all Africans were originally Muslim; Christianity, which most African-Americans then professed, was a tool of "white devils" to subjugate them. Rather than seeking equality and integration, Fard preferred a totally segregated, Apartheid-like system where Blacks would have their own country. Many saw his message as the way out of poverty and oppression, and he gained many followers.

In 1931, Fard met Elijah Poole (who took the name Elijah Muhammad) and trained him for over three years before Fard mysteriously disappeared. Elijah Muhammad took over leadership, and the organization continued to grow, later attracting such celebrities as Muhammad Ali and Kareem Abdul-Jabbar. Elijah Muhammad taught that W. D. Fard was Allah in the flesh, the Messiah and the Mahdi, and gave him the title of The Master. He claimed he'd been called by The Master to be the true religion's final Messenger.

As the teachings of the Nation became more widely known, it was feared by whites and watched by the government because of its nationalistic goals. Elijah Muhammad scorned the Civil Rights Movement, believing integration with whites was a denial of Black supremacy. But there were internal disputes as well. As followers began to travel and encounter Muslims outside the U.S., Malcolm X, one of the Nation's best-known spokesmen, and Elijah's own son Wallace Muhammad, began to move toward orthodox Islam and openly question some of their leader's teachings. Elihah Muhammad in turn began to "correct" some orthodox Islamic teachings and claimed they'd misunderstood or misinterpreted the Qur'an (while he had the true understanding).

Areas of difference with orthodox Islam are many. As to the belief that W. D. Fard was Allah incarnate, orthodox Islam denies that God has ever appeared in the flesh. Elijah Muhammad's claim to be Messenger and Prophet called of God (he also said the Bible and the Qur'an both say another scripture will come at the end times) counters the Qur'an's teaching that

Muhammad of seventh-century Arabia was the final prophet. Contrary to Islam, Christianity, and most other religions, the Nation of Islam denies any physical afterlife. Elijah Muhammad famously said, "When you are dead, you are DEAD." He used the term *resurrection* to refer to the mental awakening of Black people; the goal of this belief system is to produce a heaven on earth for Black people, not to prepare them for another life after this one. That contradicts both the Qur'an and the Bible, a problem he handled by declaring that both books had been tampered with and therefore contain errors.

Followers of the Nation of Islam are often called "Black Muslims," a term that can be misleading. At face value, it refers to any Muslim of African descent, regardless of current dwelling. However, the number of orthodox Muslims in Africa and of African descent living elsewhere easily exceeds one hundred million, far outnumbering followers of the Nation of Islam. Even in the U.S., orthodox African-American Muslims probably outnumber those who belong to the Nation, though exact numbers are hard to determine. The term is intended to communicate that they follow an Islamic form that's only for people of African descent. While it was originally considered just for African-Americans, now it has spread to some parts of the African continent. In South Africa, ironically, they advocate for a return to the Apartheid arrangement, with independent, segregated Black homelands.

After Elijah Muhammad's death in 1975, several years of controversy and leadership turmoil brought declining numbers and financial problems. In 1978, The Honorable Minister Louis Farrakhan (his official title) took over the struggling group, pledging to restore the teachings of Elijah Muhammad. A highly gifted orator, Farrakhan's early years were characterized by fiery speeches denouncing whites, Christianity, and the government. Following the teachings of his predecessor, he claimed God hates whites and had intended Black people to rule the world. He has written extensively, publishing books and magazines promoting the Nation's views. He restored financial stability, and the organization began to grow again. In more recent years his speeches have been less hostile, and he has been more willing to work with other organizations (e.g., NAACP, Black churches) toward common goals.

While not repudiating the teachings of Elijah Muhammad, Farrakhan has slowly moved the group closer to orthodox Islam, even suggesting joint conferences and other public gatherings. He followed up the Million Man March success with the Millions More Movement (seeking to move more African-Americans out of poverty and crime), with which they've had some success. Current official statements from the Nation of Islam show little change in beliefs or attitudes. While demanding equality, quality education, and an end to discrimination, they continue to press for a separate nation for Black people.

An Extra Minute

At least part of the Nation of Islam's teaching is bucking a national trend. One official statement condemns racial intermarriage or any racial mixing; recent statistics show that nearly 15 percent of all marriages in the U.S. are between people of differing ethnicities, and the trend is growing rapidly. Integration of all ethnic groups may eventually occur through biology rather than law.

Baha'i

The newest of what are generally considered world religions is Baha'i, which only began in the mid-nineteenth century. Although small, with about six million followers, in less than one hundred fifty years it has become a global and growing religion with adherents in almost every country.

Baha'i began in what is now Iran and was first seen as a sect of Shi'ite Islam. Shi'ites believe that one of the great imams of the past (some Shi'ites believe there were seven imams, others twelve) is still alive, in hiding, and one day will reveal himself as the Mahdi, who will bring worldwide peace and justice. In 1844, Ali Muhammad declared himself to be the twelfth imam and took the name *Bab-ud-Din*, meaning "Gate of Faith." Great excitement and rejoicing turned to anger and persecution when Bab-ud-Din's teachings turned out to be inconsistent with the Qur'an. He was executed in 1850, along with many of his followers, but predicted before his death that another man would come after him who would establish a new religion.

Those followers who were not killed were exiled to Baghdad, where in 1863, one of them, Husayn Ali, proclaimed he was the foretold one and took the name *Bahaullah*, meaning "glory of God." Those who believed him took the name Baha'i. This group was forcibly moved around the Middle East for years until eventually arriving in Acre, near present-day Haifa, Israel.

Bahaullah was imprisoned the rest of his life, but wrote a number of books and letters and sent out missionaries to spread his message. When he died in 1892, he was succeeded by his son Abbas Effendi, who took the name *Abdul Baha*, meaning "Servant of Baha." He continued his father's work of writing, was released from prison in 1908, and began to travel widely in Europe and North America, proclaiming the Baha'i message and organizing local assemblies of followers. Baha'i leadership passed to his grandson Shoghi Effendi in 1921, who continued this work until his death in 1957. Thereafter, leadership ceased to be hereditary and was handed over to an elected body chosen from the now global Baha'i community.

The basics of Baha'i belief began with Bab-ud-Din, but it was the prolific writer Bahaullah who organized and articulated the faith in several books and other writings. Baha'is believe that all religions come from the same source and that revelation is progressive through a kind of spiritual evolution. As humanity has progressed, God has sent different messengers with additional revelation. Therefore, all prophets, and all religious scriptures, have some truth, and each new prophet's teachings build on that of the previous ones. Among the named prophets are Moses, Zoroaster (Zarathustra), Buddha, Jesus, and Muhammad. Unlike Muhammad, who claimed to be the final prophet, Bahaullah said other prophets would come after him as humanity became sufficiently developed to receive further revelation.

Central to the Baha'i belief system is the oneness, or unity, of humanity. A major emphasis springing from this is their work for world peace. In 1920, Abdul Baha was given the Order of the British Empire for his work in promoting world peace. Even before the League of Nations was formed following World War I, Baha'is advocated for the establishment of a world tribunal for peacefully settling global disputes. Some would even prefer a world government and the elimination of all national boundaries, believing that national pride and greed have led to many wars. Another is the creation of a universal language to aid communication between nations. Baha'is were early advocates of Esperanto, a language created to be easy to learn (it has no exceptions to its grammar rules) and politically and culturally neutral. Some U.S. high schools included Esperanto in their foreign language offerings between the 1950s and 1970s, but it never became popular and has nearly faded from public knowledge today.

Other Baha'i values also support the beliefs above. They were early advocates for compulsory public education. While not suggesting everyone should live at the same socioeconomic level, Baha'is believe that extremes of wealth and poverty should be abolished. Bahaullah did not give a specific plan or type of government he thought could best carry out that goal, preferring that the wealthy voluntarily contribute to alleviate suffering among the poor. They believe in complete equality between the sexes and condemn all prejudice of other ethnicities, religions, nations, etc.

Baha'is do not believe Satan is an actual being and reject the idea of evil as an active force. They do not believe in a literal heaven or hell, seeing those statements in the Bible and Qur'an as allegorical or adapted to an earlier, less-developed age. Instead, they believe people's souls will exist either closer to or further from God depending on their deeds in this present life. They teach the harmony of religion and science. Any differences, they say, eventually will be resolved as humans gain further knowledge.

Baha'is promote high moral standards for their followers. Use of alcohol and drugs is forbidden. All are expected to work and to see their work as an act of worship. Divorce, though permitted, is difficult to obtain and must be preceded by a yearlong attempt at reconciliation. Parents are expected to provide their children with the highest quality education possible. Baha'i is a missionary religion, and followers are expected to actively propagate their faith. They do not accept donations from non-members.

Baha'is use prescribed daily individual prayers. Corporate worship is rather informal and, depending on the size of a congregation, may be held in a home or rented facility. There is no clergy, and anyone, male or female, may speak. Readings include not only the writings of Bahaullah, but may be taken from the Bible, Qur'an, or any other religious scriptures. Prayers are recited; there is no formal sermon or teaching. Some cities with many Baha'is have magnificent buildings for worship—always nine-sided, covered with a dome.

An Extra Minute

The Baha'i emphasis on world peace and unity of all religions appeals to many and contributes to steady growth. The struggles of maintaining high moral standards in today's world create one of Baha'is' greatest challenges: that of attrition or members leaving the faith in discouragement.

Hinduism: Origins

Hinduism, the world's third largest religion, has about 850 million followers. Most Hindus live in India, although the Indian diaspora (Indians joke that the country's biggest export is people) has taken the religion around the globe. Sizeable Hindu populations live in the United Kingdom, Canada, the U.S., East Africa, and on the island of Bali in Indonesia.

Unlike most religions, Hinduism has no identifiable founder or "starting point." The available evidence suggests it has developed out of one or more ancient indigenous religious systems in India, plus outside influences brought by invaders who called themselves *Aryans*, meaning "noble ones." They entered India from what is now Iran, about 1500 BC. Even within India, the religion exhibits tremendous variety. In some ways, the label *Hinduism* is a convenient Western term, now adopted by India itself, for the great variety of Indian religious expressions. Hinduism also gave birth to three additional religions: Buddhism, Jainism, and Sikhism.

Religious expression is influenced not only by the underlying belief system but also by the culture in which it develops. This is most clearly seen in comparing faiths that began in the Middle East (Judaism, Zoroastrianism, Christianity, Islam, and Baha'i), which are all monotheistic, with those that began in India (Hinduism, Jainism, Buddhism, and Sikhism), which are, with the exception of Sikhism, polytheistic or agnostic, and far more contemplative. With Sikhism again as the exception, the monotheistic faiths believe humans live once and are judged by God after death; the others believe in reincarnation, giving humans multiple tries to improve their spiritual condition.

Hinduism is probably best known for its many gods and goddesses, represented by a huge variety of colorful statues, sometimes called idols. But this is just the surface of Hindu worship. The core beliefs that underlie all the various Hindu expressions are karma and reincarnation.

Karma is often described as "the law of cause and effect": What you sow by your deeds in this life you will reap in the next. In another life here on earth, that is, not an eternal state (monotheistic heaven or hell). And not determined by a conscious, personal God, but by an unconscious, automatic process. One might say it's just the nature of the universe, "the way things are."

In the West, karma and reincarnation have become something of a fad. Recent polls show that nearly 40 percent of Americans believe in reincarnation, and discovering what one was in a past life has become a popular pastime. At a fortunate circumstance, a person will joke that they "must have had some good karma." But in Hinduism, where the concepts come from, reincarnation is a curse to be escaped. And because karma is what keeps a person chained to the wheel of endless deaths and rebirths, all karma is bad. The ultimate goal of a Hindu, though rarely expected "this time around," is to avoid all karma and achieve *moksha,* "a state of oneness with the ultimate reality," called Brahman.

Brahman, though sometimes referred to as God, is imper-sonal, indefinable, unknowable, unmanifested, and without attributes. It is sometimes described as the sum of everything that exists. In Hindu belief, we are all Brahman, but thinking we have our own individual identity keeps us on the reincarna-tion wheel. Only after we realize we are Brahman (some Hindus would say we realize we are God) do we escape another rebirth. An analogy some Hindus use for entering Nirvana is that of squeezing a drop from a medicine dropper into the ocean.

This belief in one ultimate reality is called *monism*, which means "all of reality is of one kind or nature." For Hindus, all reality is spiritual; the physical universe is just an illusion. Part of recognizing oneness with Brahman is recognizing that the physical body and the world are not real. Most religions believe both the spiritual (metaphysical) and the material (physical) exist and are different from each other in important ways. The other monistic belief system, although not usually thought of as a religion, is Secular Humanism, which holds that only the material universe exists; there is no spiritual reality.

Hindus, by their own calculation, worship more than 330 mil-lion gods and goddesses. How does this fit with the monistic worldview? The average Indian villager knows nothing of monism. He or she worships local deities (and perhaps one or two higher gods, such as Shiva or Ganesh—see chapter 22) and accepts further reincarnation as inevitable. The hope is to have as little karma as possible so that next time they might be born into a higher caste. The educated or philosophical Hindu explains this apparent dis-crepancy as all being part of the illusion. The myriad gods are just facets of Brahman. None represents all of reality. So Hinduism is both monistic and polytheistic, and in some rural areas it continues also to retain some animistic beliefs and practices.

The current Hindu belief system did not develop through the teaching of one individual or an organized scriptural narrative with claims to having been revealed by God. The oldest Hindu scriptures, the *Vedas*, consist of four collections of ancient hymns, rituals, and chants, written in an early form of Sanskrit. They probably were composed around 1500 BC and passed down orally for centuries, then put into written form more than a thousand years later.

All we can learn of ancient Hindu beliefs about their gods is implied from the content of the hymns of praise to their deities. Many of the gods mentioned in the Vedas are no longer worshiped today. The last sections of each Veda are called the *Upanishads*, which are philosophical reflections on life that likely were added much later. While the Vedas clearly reflect polytheistic beliefs, the Upanishads are usually monistic in nature.

Also important in Hindu literature are several epic poems. These tell stories (much like folklore) that help us understand ancient Indian life and the religious beliefs and practices that shaped it. The most famous is the *Bhagavad Gita*, contained within a longer epic called the *Mahabharata*. The great battle it describes has been dramatized for Indian television and remains popular year after year (like a soap opera). In it, a king struggles with facing the horrors of war. His chariot driver, Krishna, an incarnation of the god Vishnu, tells him his dharma requires him to fight the enemy. The *Ramayana* is another popular epic poem about Vishnu and his consort Lakshmi.

An Extra Minute

Adolf Hitler adopted the label *Aryan*, "noble or superior one," for the master-race concept on which Nazism was built. He also borrowed the swastika from Hinduism, where it is a symbol of reincarnation, and utilized it to instill terror in Germany's enemies (not because he believed in reincarnation).

Hinduism: Beliefs and Practices

As mentioned in chapter 21, Hindu practice involves the worship of a vast multitude of deities. Worship consists primarily of prayers (usually chanted) and praise songs, plus offerings of food, milk, or money placed in front of a statue or idol of the god being worshiped. Worship, both corporate and individual, may take place in a temple. Some temples are dedicated to one god while others contain statues representing a number of gods. Most Hindu homes have shrines as well, with pictures or smaller statues to represent the gods chosen for worship by that family. No one attempts to worship all 330 million gods; people choose a few that are important to a person's family, caste, occupation, or circumstances.

Hinduism has an elaborate hierarchical structure for both gods and humans. At the top are *Brahma*, the Creator (different from Brahman, ultimate reality); *Shiva*, the Destroyer (also the god of fertility); and *Vishnu*, the Preserver. These three together are called the *Trimurti*, which some Hindus believe represents three facets of Brahman and thus sometimes mistakenly equate with the Christian Trinity.

The statues that represent these and the other gods and goddesses are usually in somewhat human form, but there are exceptions. The popular *Ganesh,* god of business and prosperity, is depicted as having the head of an elephant on a human body. *Hanuman* has the body and face of a monkey. Most gods have wives or consorts, and some of these goddesses have become popular enough to have their own temples and devotees. *Lakshmi*, goddess of wealth and good fortune, is the spouse of Vishnu. *Kali*, consort of Shiva, is usually depicted wearing a necklace of human skulls. The city of Calcutta (literally, *Kali khat*) is named after her.

Vishnu is a god of benevolence and love, who is believed to sometimes appear on earth to help people. Since long before video games, the cyber world, and the cinema made it a household word, *avatar* was the term used for these appearances in various forms. *Krishna*, mentioned in the *Bhagavad Gita,* is believed to be one of Vishnu's avatars. Among Hindus, *Gautama*, who became the Buddha, also is thought to be an avatar of Vishnu. According to Hindu legend, Vishnu has appeared nine times already and will appear once more, riding on a white horse, when he comes to judge the world.

For humans, the hierarchy is called *caste.* Everyone is born into a family that belongs to one, and they remain in this caste their entire lives. It is believed that karma (from deeds done in the previous life) determines one's caste in the present life. There are several thousand castes based on occupation, but they are grouped into four major categories. The *Brahmins,* the priests, are the highest and smallest caste. *Kshatriyas* are rulers and warriors. The *Vaishyas* are merchants and landowner farmers. The *Shudras* are laborers, subdivided into many categories of work. And, at the very bottom, *below* the four main categories, are the *Dalits*, traditionally called Untouchables for being so ritually unclean that even their shadow falling on a high-caste person causes defilement. Dalits are often physically unclean as well, since they have to do the dirtiest jobs and usually are denied access to community wells. Marrying someone from a different caste is still quite rare in India.

In theory, the Hindu goal is to achieve moksha and escape reincarnation, but most Hindus, except some Brahmins, have no hope of that and think more in terms of how to be reborn into a higher caste. One does this by reducing or eliminating karma by following the dharma for one's caste. *Dharma*, often translated as "duty," defines what is expected of each caste. A common statement is "It is a king's dharma to rule and it is a stone's dharma to be hard." Central to the dharma for lower castes is that they serve the upper castes without envy. Trying to improve one's position in life is denying dharma and results in amassing even more bad karma. Plainly this system is a major barrier to social change and improvement and is very controversial in contemporary India.

Although most Hindus only pray to their gods about daily needs and desires, some practice prayer devotedly and work hard to progress toward moksha. Hinduism offers multiple paths by which this progress may be obtained. By far the most common is devotion to a particular god; the most popular gods are Shiva and Krishna. Those who devote themselves to one deity believe that particular god encompasses all facets of Brahman, and through sincere worship this god may be inclined to help the worshiper achieve release from reincarnation. Another path is asceticism, an attempt at detachment from all worldly desires. In India, it's still common to see *sadhus,* or holy men, wandering the streets and roads, clothed in a simple cloth, carrying only a begging bowl for food. A third path is meditation. This is more often associated with Buddhism, yet some Hindus focus on the inner self to find oneness with Brahman. The fourth path, quite rare today, is animal sacrifice. This method is a remnant holdover from the ancient religion of the Aryan invaders.

One Hindu doctrine is *ahimsa,* meaning "non-injury to life." This is the reason most Hindus are vegetarian. In the animal hierarchy, the cow is at the top, so even those who don't keep a strict vegetarian diet usually avoid beef. For the higher castes, even touching leather brings defilement; the handling of animal carcasses is left to the Dalits.

An Extra Minute

A Hindu man owns a number of the Burger King franchises in Minnesota. When asked how he could run businesses that consume beef, he replied, "Religion has its dharma, and business has its dharma."

Hinduism: Today

We've already seen that Hinduism displays tremendous variety even in India. India's place at the forefront of twenty-first-century globalization and modernization has impacted religious practice, as well. Rural life mostly has gone on as it has for centuries, despite the introduction of radio and television, but in cities, a burgeoning middle class is being changed by the secularizing influences of Westernization. India, a nuclear power, is noted for its progress in science and technology. It's also the world's largest democracy, and the political aspirations of its people sometimes clash with Hindu values.

This clash is most evident today in the social and economic aspirations of the Dalits (Untouchables). For centuries given the lowest jobs, they achieved legal rights at India's independence from Great Britain in 1947. Mahatma Gandhi called them *harijan*, "children of God," and India's constitution outlawed the caste system, but just as 1960s Civil Rights laws didn't eliminate racial prejudice in the U.S., discrimination against Dalits has continued. India has a form of affirmative action that has guaranteed a percentage of university admissions and government jobs to each caste, and there are Dalits who have earned PhDs, but they are still denied entry into many hotels and restaurants (the upper castes believe their presence would bring defilement).

For devout Hindus, the Dalits are born into their state due to karma from a previous life—to seek improvement is to only make things worse next time around. Some Dalits have protested against Hinduism entirely by formally and publicly converting to Christianity or, more recently, Buddhism. The caste issue is still challenging traditional Hindu beliefs, and change is slow. Cross-caste marriages are slowly being accepted among the educated, urban population, but in rural areas they can still result in so-called honor killings.

As Indians have migrated to many parts of the world over the centuries, this diversity of religious expression has increased even more. While Indians in East Africa, Guyana, and Bali live fairly traditional lives and have seen little change in religious practices, those who have migrated to the U.K., the U.S., and Canada face cultural pressures of many types. Lifestyles are busier, with less time for communal worship. Public education is a secularizing influence on children. The cost of land in large cities makes the construction of temples difficult, and travel distances may be prohibitive. Even so, Hindus in the West continue to practice their faith. The second largest *Divali* (an important Hindu holiday) celebration in the world is held in Leicester, England—ironically, the birthplace of William Carey, the first English missionary to India.

One adaptation immigrant Indians have made is in building multipurpose temples that service a broad spectrum of the Hindu community. The largest Hindu temple in the U.S., in Maple Grove, Minnesota, has seven distinct sections so that devotees of different gods can worship in the same facility. Many former church buildings have been turned into Hindu temples after Christian congregations disband, merge, or move to the suburbs. Through a variety of means, diaspora Hindus find ways to practice their faith.

Most Hindus make no effort to proselytize. Generally they see karma as universal; if a person is born into a Muslim or Christian family, that is their dharma and that's what they should remain this time around. Other religions are, for them, just a few more of the three-thousand-plus castes. Because Hinduism itself has such variety, encompassing polytheism, monism, and even a form of monotheism, it easily adopts other faiths; Muslim, Christian, Sikh, Jain, and Buddhist minorities have lived in India for centuries.

But there have been exceptions. Not long ago a Hindu Nationalist party won a majority of seats in India's Parliament. Their platform, in simplified terms: "India is for Hindus only. Convert or leave." The government turned a blind eye as Hindu mobs torched mosques and churches, beating, raping, and killing Muslims and Christians. An international outcry was heard after Graham Staines, an Australian Christian missionary who cared for lepers, was burned alive along with his young sons. Most Hindus were as outraged as everyone else by the violence; the Hindu Nationalist party eventually was voted out of office. Some tensions remain, and there are still occasional outbreaks, but persecution of non-Hindus has subsided in recent years.

A few forms of Hinduism do seek to propagate the faith and encourage conversions. The Vedanta Society, teaching a highly philosophical and monistic form of Hinduism, has sent missionaries to the West since the nineteenth century and has centers in most large North American and European cities. Better known because of their street witnessing and public singing and chanting are followers of Hare Krishna. There have been devotees of Krishna ever since the *Bhagavad Gita* was written, but this group gained prominence in recent decades and began to send missionaries to the West. Hare Krishna groups outside India today are composed primarily of converts and have very few ethnic Indians.

Hindu belief (if not organized Hinduism) has spread even more widely in the West through Transcendental Meditation and New Age religions. TM claims to be nonreligious, but its practices are based on a *yogic* form of Hinduism. *Yoga*, now a popular form of stress relief and exercise, comes from a Sanskrit word meaning "yoke" and in Hinduism is used to yoke or join the practitioner with Brahman. (We'll discuss New Age religions in chapter 39.)

An Extra Minute

It's been said that while Islam has won more converts in the West, Hinduism has had a far greater influence on how we think and has, therefore, impacted more people. One clear example is the 40 percent of Americans who now believe in reincarnation. This would have been unthinkable as recently as the 1970s. Hinduism may seem to be "over there" in India, but it has become a truly global religion.

24

Jainism

Jainism, little known in the West, had a significant role in shaping post-classical Hinduism. And although today it has barely four million followers, Jainism continues to have an impact on modern India because its adherents are among the wealthiest and most influential of the country's businessmen.

The founder was a man named Mahavira, born somewhere around 590 BC into the Kshatriya caste. As a young man, he abandoned his life of wealth and ease and joined a group of Hindu ascetics in search of answers to life's deep questions. He found even their self-deprivation insufficient and set out on his own course of extreme asceticism, seeking the most difficult and painful circumstances to free his soul from the bonds of reincarnation. After twelve years, he claimed to have achieved moksha (release) and spent his remaining thirty or so years teaching others about the path he had discovered.

Unlike the monistic concept of Hinduism, Mahavira taught the dualism of body and soul. Somewhat like the ancient Greek philosophers, he saw the body, or material universe, as evil and the soul as good. Karma holds the soul onto the wheel of re-incarnation "like mud clings to a wheel." If this is so, the only solution is extreme asceticism, depriving the body to weaken its grip on the soul. The goal becomes complete detachment from worldly things.

Mahavira also placed great emphasis on *ahimsa*, the doctrine of non-injury to life. He would only accept leftover food, not wanting to be the cause of death to any living thing. Jain monks typically sweep the path in front of them as they walk, wear a mask over their nose and mouth, and strain their drinking water in order to avoid injury even to an insect. Today most Jains practice what they call "pure vegetarianism," not only abstaining from all meat but also refusing eggs (which might be fertilized) or anything that grows under the surface of the ground (like potatoes or carrots).

Jainism is atheistic in practice, if not in absolute doctrine. If any gods exist, said Mahavira, they are in a different sphere of reality and are of no use to humans, who must find moksha by their own efforts, not by depending on supernatural help. Therefore, gods are irrelevant and any question of their existence is pointless. A visitor to a Jain temple would see twenty-four statues, with people making small offerings and praying in front of them, similar to what one would see in a Hindu temple. Jains are quick to explain, however, that these statues do not represent gods or goddesses. They believe Mahavira was the last of twenty-four *Tirthankaras*, meaning "crossing builders." These were men of wisdom and insight who helped show people the way to "cross over" from the material world to the realm of the soul. Jains venerate the Tirthankaras but do not worship them.

Some scholars think Mahavira's goal, at least initially, was to reform Hinduism rather than to start a new religion. He lived in a period of great discontent with the established order. Today, we say "information is power," and in an era when few could read, while the Hindu scriptures were in an ancient language only the Brahmins knew, the priests had abused their high position and become wealthy and powerful at society's expense. Mahavira rejected the authority of the Vedas, believing they were not sacred scripture. He also taught that a person of any caste could attain moksha by following his path of asceticism. Hindu teaching was that only Brahmin males had any hope of escaping reincarnation. Mahavira further believed in a more egalitarian (if not democratic) society.

Not surprisingly, the Hindu establishment opposed Jain doctrines. While over the centuries they occasionally have persecuted the Jains, Hinduism was influenced by Mahavira's teachings. Asceticism became one of the paths to moksha; ahimsa became more strongly followed; many priestly abuses were curbed. As Hinduism changed and adapted, most of Mahavira's followers were reabsorbed into Hinduism, and the Jains have remained a tiny minority religion to this day.

Several centuries after Mahavira's death, the Jains began to split over what constituted true Jainism. During the first century BC, they divided into two sects. The *Digambara* ("sky clad") are the smaller and more conservative group. Their monks wander without clothing, and they believe women have no hope of achieving moksha. The *Svetambara* ("white clad") monks wear a simple cloth, and this larger group allows women into its monasteries, believing they also might achieve moksha.

About six thousand of Jainism's four million adherents are actual monks who practice extreme asceticism. The rest assume moksha will happen in another life and accept their reincarnation as inevitable. Due to Mahavira's emphasis on ahimsa and belief that all action accumulates karma, Jains tend to work in business, accounting, and related fields that involve less physical activity. Ironically, the followers of a religion emphasizing asceticism and poverty have become one of India's wealthiest groups.

An Extra Minute

Mahavira lived during the sixth century BC. This was an amazing window in religious history, since Siddhartha Gautama (the Buddha), Confucius, Lao-tzu, and the Hebrew prophets Isaiah, Jeremiah, and Ezekiel also lived, taught, and wrote during this time, sometimes called the "axis age" of religion. With the possible exception of the prophets, there is no indication any of these men knew one another or were aware of the others' teachings. It is fascinating to imagine what a conversation among them all might have been like.

Sikhism

Traditional Sikh men are recognizable by their starched, symmetrical turbans and full beards. Because Sikhs are not to cut their hair, older men's beards and hair are piled on top of the head, under the turban. A few Hindus and some types of Muslims also wear turbans, though of a different style. This led to a tragic case of mistaken identity in the first reprisal killing after September 11, 2001, when an enraged American murdered a Sikh store owner in Phoenix, assuming anyone wearing a turban was Muslim.

The Sikh religion is unique in attempting to synthesize one religion out of two very different ones. Nanak, its founder, was born into a Hindu family during the late fifteenth century in the Punjab region of northwest India. This was during the period of the Moghul Empire, when a Muslim minority ruled over the Hindu majority.

Besides his Hindu upbringing, Nanak was highly influenced by a Muslim teacher. He apparently had a contemplative personality and spent much time reflecting on religion. At about age thirty, he claimed to receive a revelation from God while meditating. He was called to be a prophet of the true religion and preach the message of the essential unity of Islam and Hinduism.

For the next several decades, Nanak wandered India, teaching his concepts and organizing communities wherever people accepted his message. These followers were called *Sikhs*, a Punjabi word meaning "disciple." Nanak taught that there is only one God, called The True Name. Hindu polytheism, he said, just sees many different facets of this one God. Also similar to Islam, he believed in the duality of the universe, the reality of both the material and spiritual worlds. The earth was created by God; humans are the pinnacle of that creation. From Hinduism, Nanak retained the concepts of karma and reincarnation and taught that The True Name would eventually free humans from the cycle of rebirths. He also taught very simple forms of worship, rejecting most of the rituals of both religions.

Despite rejection and occasional persecution, Nanak was a pacifist and never retaliated or sought revenge. He was given the title Guru Nanak. To Hindus, a *guru* is a teacher or guide, but to Sikhs, the word means "leader." Guru Nanak continued to teach, compose hymns, and organize the Sikh community until his death in 1552. He was followed by nine more gurus. The first three continued to promote his nonviolent emphasis, but as the Sikh community grew and its teaching became more widely known, they faced increasing opposition from the Muslim rulers of northern India. Many Sikh gurus were imprisoned and executed. Beginning with the fifth leader, Guru Arjan, the Sikhs became more militant, taking up arms and defending themselves against persecutors. Guru Arjan also compiled the writings of the previous gurus into the *Granth*, the Sikh scriptures.

The Sikhs became excellent warriors, calling themselves *Singhs*, which means "lion" in Punjabi (most Sikhs have the last name Singh). The Muslim rulers continued to target Sikh leadership, however, and since the assassination of the tenth guru, Gobind Singh, in 1708, the Sikhs have looked to the Granth for leadership rather than a human guru. When the British colonized India, they employed the Sikhs as soldiers and policemen, vocations in which they continue to predominate in modern, independent India.

Sikh worship consists primarily of prayers and hymns. There are no priests, and anyone with knowledge can lead worship. Corporate gatherings are held in the *gurdwara,* which has characteristics of both Muslim and Hindu worship spaces. Like a mosque, the main worship room has no furniture, just mats or carpets on the floor, and the scriptures are prominently displayed on an ornate stand. Although there are no idols, large portraits of the ten gurus hang on the walls. An integral part of corporate worship is the communal meal at the end. Even non-Sikhs visiting a gurdwara are encouraged to accept their hospitality and join in the meal. Many gurdwaras also have sleeping facilities any traveler is welcome to use.

Sikhs, like other Indians, have migrated all over the world. Gurdwaras can be found in most major European and North American cities. And though they can be found throughout India, most Sikhs continue to live in Punjab, the country's breadbasket. The geographic center of the Sikh religion is the Golden Temple, a magnificent building in Amritsar, Punjab's principle city. Although Sikhism rejects the Hindu concept of caste, Sikhs still tend toward certain vocations. In addition to soldiering and policing, they are most often found in occupations related to transportation (e.g., airline pilots, railroad engineers, taxi drivers).

As mentioned, most Sikhs have the family name Singh and belong to mainstream Sikhism. The religion has, however, produced two small splinter groups. *Udasis* are ascetic holy men who wander the villages and cities, wearing only a simple cloth and carrying their begging bowl for sustenance. *Sahajdaris* focus more on the pacifist teachings of the early gurus. They also are generally clean-shaven rather than bearded.

Conversion is rare, but a few Europeans and North Americans, attracted to the religion's simplicity, have converted. Sikhs number about nineteen million, making them a small minority in today's India. In fact, the country now has more Christians than Sikhs. This has produced a nationalist movement among the Sikh community who believe the state of Punjab should become an independent country. Some of these nationalists have adopted terrorist tactics, attacking government buildings and installations.

An Extra Minute

The 2002 movie *Bend It Like Beckham* concerns a Sikh family that has immigrated to the United Kingdom. The British-born daughter struggles between her traditional parents and the Western culture in which she has grown up. The father, consistent with Sikh vocational preferences, is an airline pilot. The movie features Keira Knightley and Jonathan Rhys Meyers, but the director and most of the other actors, including the main character, are Sikhs.

Theravada Buddhism

Buddhism is the fourth largest of the world's religions, with about 350 million followers, and like Hinduism, its influence extends far beyond the actual numbers. Theravada, the most traditional, conservative form, today is found primarily in Sri Lanka and Southeast Asia. Although some of its followers intermingle animistic beliefs and practices, Theravada is essentially nontheistic, believing that enlightenment must be achieved by one's own efforts, without supernatural assistance. Since Theravada is closest to the original, Buddhism's beginnings will be described in this chapter.

Buddhism began in India, though now it is a tiny minority there. Like Jainism, which began at about the same time, it started as a reform movement within Hinduism but developed into a separate religion. Siddhartha Gautama, its founder, was born into the family of a Kshatriya raja (minor ruler). Many legends have developed regarding his life, and sorting fact from later additions is difficult. Generally accepted dates for his life are 560–480 BC.

According to tradition, at his birth it was foretold that if he saw only beauty and youth he would become a great king, but if he saw disease and death he would become a religious teacher. Since his father preferred the former outcome, Gautama grew up in an extremely sheltered environment, rarely leaving the walls of his palace. He married and had a son, but around age thirty became restless with his confined life. He slipped out and, deeply disturbed by seeing sick and dead people in the area, left his family and took up the life of a wandering monk. He tried philosophy, then the most extreme forms of asceticism. One legend claims that during this period he lived on one daily grain of rice. However, even this did not bring him the answers he sought. He gave up asceticism, ate a meal, and sat under the shade of a tree to meditate. Finally, through meditation, Gautama found enlightenment and became the Buddha, meaning "Enlightened One."

The Buddha was about thirty-five when he was so illuminated, and spent the rest of his life spreading his teaching and gathering disciples. He rejected the authority of the Vedas and said both men and women from any caste had the potential to attain enlightenment. Unlike Jainism, which saw most early followers reabsorbed into Hinduism while bringing reforms to the larger faith, the Buddha's followers quickly separated from the parent religion.

Like the other Indian faiths, Buddhism accepted karma and reincarnation; life's goal was to become free of the endless cycle (birth, death, and rebirth). But whereas Hinduism believes ultimate reality is the sum of everything, the Buddha taught that ultimate reality is a void, or Nothingness. The Hindu goal of moksha, "oneness with Brahman," is replaced with Nirvana, "extinguishing" or "ceasing to exist." While this might not seem appealing in today's prosperous Western world, if life truly *is* suffering, as Buddhism teaches, then not having to return to it again and again is indeed preferable.

During his period of meditation, the Buddha developed what he called the Four Noble Truths:

1. Life consists of suffering and pain.
2. Suffering exists because of desire.
3. The way to end suffering is ceasing to desire or crave things.
4. The way to cease desiring is to follow the Eightfold Path (often called the Middle Way because it avoids both extremes of indulgence and asceticism).

The steps on this path are:

1. Right view
2. Right intention
3. Right speech
4. Right action
5. Right livelihood
6. Right effort
7. Right mindfulness
8. Right concentration

The teachings of the Buddha, as written down by his disciples, elaborate on this Eightfold Path, and it is believed that following it properly will result in enlightenment and release from reincarnation.

Buddhism's spread was greatly aided by the 297 BC conversion of Asoka, who thirty years later became India's emperor. This commitment was significant, and Asoka used the royal treasury to fund the sending of Buddhist missionaries to places outside India. There are claims that they traveled as far west as Greece, but it is to the east that Buddhism found its new home, receiving rapid acceptance in Ceylon (present-day Sri Lanka) and Burma. As Buddhism dwindled to a small minority in its birthplace, its eastward growth continued into Southeast Asia and China and eventually Korea and Japan.

As Theravada Buddhism holds that enlightenment can be achieved only through human effort, its temples are for meditation and reflection rather than worship. Gautama said that if gods did exist, they lived in a different sphere of existence and had their own karma to deal with. They were of no benefit to humans; there was no point in being concerned about or worshiping them.

Since the Eightfold Path requires profound discipline and commitment, few follow it consistently. The monks live out the ideal Buddhist life, and laypeople support the monks. Over the years, Buddhism has developed a concept of merit, or good karma, which is supposed to improve one's spiritual life in the next reincarnation; supporting the monks is thought to help a person gain more merit. In Thailand, young men are expected to spend one or two years living a monk life's before they marry and settle down. It is important to the family that they do this, since the merit they gain through this service is believed to benefit them all. The monks' practices are intended to avoid all karma, good or bad, for any karma is a barrier to enlightenment and Nirvana.

As Buddhism has spread it has adapted and changed in many ways. Some of these variations will be described in chapters 27–28.

An Extra Minute

A common question: "If the Buddha was first an ascetic, then practiced moderation, why do statues of him show a fat person?" The answer: The small statues seen in Asian businesses are not Buddha statues but representations of the god of prosperity, meant to bring good luck in commerce.

Mahayana Buddhism

Early in Buddhism's development, disputes about the correct meaning of Gautama's teaching divided his followers into various schools of thought. Within ten years of his death, there were sixteen different factions. Several councils, one convened by Emperor Asoka, attempted to bring unity but failed. Over the next several centuries, these groups organized themselves, elaborated on their doctrinal views, and deepened what became permanent divisions.

The *Hinayana* ("exclusive way") groups were more conservative; today Theravada is the only remaining Hinayana branch. The *Mahayana* ("expansive way") schools, largely because of their flexibility in accommodating other religions, were more successful in their missionary efforts and now are Buddhism's largest branch. Various types of Mahayana Buddhism are found in China, Korea, Japan, and other parts of Asia.

Central to the Mahayana system is the belief that in addition to what he taught publicly, the Buddha gave a number of secret or hidden teachings to a select and qualified few. This idea gave authority to additions and changes as the movement spread and developed. One of the first was that Gautama was more than a man. This deification of Buddha as an eternal being who came to help humankind led to Buddhism's decline in India, even while helping it spread elsewhere. Hindus simply adopted Gautama as one of Vishnu's ten avatars, and by encouraging his worship, drew devotees back into Hinduism.

This deification also led to the teaching that Gautama was not the only Buddha. As Buddhist missionaries entered a new area and began to teach, they did not reject or condemn the region's gods, but merely taught that these also were incarnations of Buddha, and the local religion could continue while Buddhist principles were added. This was especially effective in China. By the time Buddhist missionaries arrived, about AD 200, worship cults had grown up around Confucius and Lao-tzu (the founder of Taoism), so their god status was already accepted. Buddhism lent justification to the idea that these men were more than human, no matter their own teaching to the contrary.

Another key Mahayana addition concerns beings called *Bodhisattvas*. These are humans who become enlightened, but have taken a vow to delay entering Nirvana to use their excess merit for helping others find enlightenment. Some believe the Bodhisattvas will do this until everyone has reached Nirvana. Whatever the variations, Bodhisattvas have become objects of devotion to Mahayana adherents, as they are believed to answer the prayers of those who call on them for help.

As Buddhism spread throughout Asia, it developed a number of forms and variations in belief. As followers gathered around particular teachers, they gradually organized into sects, or denominations. Often these take on some characteristics of the culture in which they develop. In places like Tibet and Bhutan, geographic isolation has produced unique Buddhist forms. Some of these sects have become quite popular; several of the Chinese and Japanese ones have active missionary movements seeking converts both in the West and from other Buddhist sects.

One of the most popular is Pure Land, which has spread to the West and adopted some Christian practices, such as Sunday schools for the instruction of children. Mahayana says there are many Buddhas and Bodhisattvas, and in this pantheon, one Buddha is Amitabha, who presides over a beautiful, blissful place called the Pure Land. Here, without evil, one may acquire Buddha-like qualities and eventually attain Nirvana. His followers believe that to enter they must live a virtuous life and repeat his name many times each day. Pure Land monks may marry and have families, like the laity. Corporate worship is church-like, with sermons and prayers to Amitabha.

Of a number of intuitive Buddhist sects, the best known is Zen, the Japanese form. Looking to Gautama's example of finding enlightenment while meditating under a tree, Zen and the other such sects place little or no emphasis on studying the Buddhist scriptures, but believe enlightenment will come through a sudden flash of insight during meditation. The beginnings of intuitive Buddhism are attributed to an Indian monk named Bodhidharma, who traveled to China as a missionary about AD 470. There are many legends about his life, one being that he cut off his own eyelids in order to stay awake longer in meditation. It is also claimed he introduced tea to China. Whether or not this is true, it is known that tea was brought from India to China around this time. Intuitive Buddhists often use highly caffeinated tea to stay awake.

Zen and most intuitive sects distrust reason and believe rational thought must be suspended for insight to occur. To aid in this, Zen has developed hundreds, perhaps thousands, of riddles called *koans,* which have no logical answer; perhaps best known in the West is "What is the sound of one hand clapping?" Zen has had much influence on Japanese art and architecture.

In contrast to the intuitive sects, in the sixth century AD, a Chinese monk named Chih-I developed a rationalistic approach to the enlightenment search that emphasized study of the Buddhist scriptures and meditation focused on careful reflection. He taught that one must study the scriptures to know the one Buddhist truth from the many different things the Buddha taught. In Japan, this form is called Tendai.

A purely Japanese sect is Nichiren, which holds that of all the Buddha's teachings, the *Lotus Sutra* is the only one necessary and is the true path to enlightenment. This sect is hostile to other forms of Buddhism and claims they are all heresies. As a result, Nichiren has faced persecution and remains relatively small. It is also very nationalistic and believes that once all of Japan has accepted its message, this form will then spread to the whole world.

An Extra Minute

Early Buddhism allowed women to become monks. This was connected to Gautama's rejection of caste, since he believed anyone, male or female, from any caste had the potential to find enlightenment and achieve Nirvana. As Buddhism was carried to other countries and adapted to those cultures, becoming a monk became limited to men.

Tibetan Buddhism

Tibetan Buddhism may be best known in the West because of the international popularity of its leader, Tenzin Gyatso, the current Dalai Lama. Tibetan Buddhist monks are called *lamas*, meaning "superior ones." There are two orders of lamas, which the West labels the Red Hats and the Yellow Hats. The Yellow Hats are the larger group and their leader is the Dalai Lama.

Buddhist missionaries entered Tibet from both India and China in the seventh century AD, at the Tibetan king's invitation. The new religion was quickly adopted and had government support. By the fourteenth century, the monks had become so powerful they took over rule and held it until the 1950 Chinese invasion. At this time, the current Dalai Lama and many followers escaped to India, where they currently live in exile. Unlike his predecessors, Tenzin Gyatso has traveled widely as a spokesman for human rights and international harmony. In 1989, he was awarded the Nobel Prize for peace.

When a Dalai Lama dies, monks thoroughly search Tibet, checking all boys born within a certain date range to see which might have the traits of the deceased leader. Further tests and divinations will be carried out to select which child is the reincarnation of the previous Dalai Lama. Then he will be taken to a monastery and given years of special training to prepare him to take over leadership of the Tibetan community. The death of this Dalai Lama will produce a special challenge, since the Tibetan community is now scattered around the globe and a search of Tibet would be hindered or forbidden by the Chinese authorities. Also, the Chinese government has said China will choose the next Dalai Lama, which most Tibetans are sure to reject. Sadly, the effort to replace a Dalai Lama noted for peace efforts may be marred by violence.

Tibetan Buddhism usually is considered a sect of the Mahayana branch, but Tibet's geographic isolation has produced a form that's quite distinct and bears little outward resemblance to the other sects. The pre-Buddhist religion of Tibet was animistic, with a strong emphasis on magic, incantations, and spells to protect people from evil spirits. Buddhism easily absorbed these practices, and one stream of Tibetan Buddhism, called *Bon*, still focuses primarily on power for this life rather than the search for enlightenment.

Tibetan Buddhism sometimes is called Tantric for of its use of *tantras*, manuals containing magical words and incantations supposed to protect the user in this life as well as help find better rebirth in the next. Tantric religion is found in other forms of Buddhism as well as a few Hindu sects. In these folk religions, the adherents may call themselves Buddhist or Hindu, but their practices more closely resemble animistic religions.

Known also to other Mahayana sects, a certain Bodhisattva named Avalokiteshvara is particularly important to Tibetan Buddhism. He is believed to have great compassion and to be able to help devotees with earthly problems as well as the search for enlightenment. His help is invoked through repeated chanting of the phrase "*Om mani padme hum.*"

A unique feature of the Tibetan form is the prayer wheel, a cylinder of various sizes containing prayers and/or incantations. Spinning or turning the cylinder is believed to repeat the prayers as if they are being spoken, thus accumulating merit for the praying person or community. Small wheels are carried by an individual and turned by hand. Larger ones may be turned by water or wind power.

When a Tibetan dies, it is believed their soul resides in a dreamlike state called *Bardo* for forty-nine days while their ultimate destiny is determined. The virtuous travel to Nirvana; karma pulls the rest into another reincarnation. The hours just preceding death are considered particularly crucial for the soul's destiny, and the monks have developed extensive rituals to help the dying achieve a better outcome.

Knowledge of Tibetan Buddhism has grown not only through the Dalai Lama's travels and speaking but also through celebrity converts like Richard Gere, Sharon Stone, Steven Seagal, Allen Ginsberg, and others. Buddhism readily adapts itself to new contexts, making it possible to hold seemingly contradictory beliefs while professing adherence. Thus, "devotees" can be accepted as Buddhist while continuing to live lavish lifestyles that would seem to be incompatible with the ethos and teachings of the Dalai Lama.

An Extra Minute

Jalue Dorjee was born in 2007, and discovered in 2009 to be a *tulku*—a reincarnated Buddhist spiritual master. According to the highest authorities of the Tibetan Buddhist order, he is the reincarnation of the speech, mind, and body of a lama (spiritual guru) who died in Switzerland in 2007. Jalue, said to be the eighth appearance of the original lama (born in 1655), was born not in India or Tibet but in Columbia Heights, Minnesota. Lamas from India have visited three times to carry out divination rituals confirming his status. Jalue will continue to live with his parents, with special attention from local Buddhist leaders, until he reaches age ten, when he will go to a monastery in India for further training.

Confucianism

Many people would describe Confucianism as a philosophy or ethical system rather than a religion. This is probably what Confucius himself intended. His writings teach about how to live and conduct oneself in this life here and now. He was personally agnostic, if not atheistic; while not directly challenging belief in gods and the supernatural, he was indifferent as to their existence—as far as he was concerned, they were irrelevant to what's really important.

But in the centuries after his death, his followers gradually folded his memory and image into the religious practices already existing in China. The Chinese prefer the term *veneration* rather than worship to describe the rituals connected with their ancestors. To the outside observer, though, the rituals would look very similar to the worship practiced by other religions. It is the inward intent that distinguishes the two concepts.

Ancient Chinese religions were polytheistic, with strong animistic elements. Gods of nature were particularly significant; local deities frequently received the most worship. The gods of a particular village or area were prayed to and offered sacrifices of food and drink on special occasions, often marked by the seasons or whenever the community experienced tragedy or blessing. These sacrifices were seen as something of an exchange: The people offered the gods something; the gods were expected to return the favor with good weather, good harvests, and good health. While the major deities were more or less permanent, if a local god failed to produce the expected blessings, he might be replaced by another deity. The local gods were also seen as part of the community and were expected to participate in local events. It was common to transport a god's statue under a canopy, to show proper respect, from the shrine to a funeral, wedding, or drama taking place in the village.

Another concept central to Chinese life—balance and harmony—is found in the principle of Yin and Yang. The Chinese believe that out of chaos, or undifferentiated potential, emerges this balance. Yin and Yang are pairs of opposites that together make up the whole of life. The Yin principle contains the feminine, darkness, cold, wetness, while the Yang is made up of the masculine, light, heat, dryness. Good and evil are not opposites in the Yin/Yang sense. A balance of Yin and Yang is good—an imbalance is evil.

And this was the norm in the time of Confucius (born 551 BC). Despite growing up in poverty, he received an education, and even as a youth showed interest in social order and government structures, which became the primary topic of his teaching and writing. His knowledge and wisdom attracted many followers, and he was able to support himself as an itinerant teacher for about thirty years. At age fifty, he became prime minister of a

Chinese province. According to legend, the government organized by his principles produced an era of near perfection, devoid of crime and highly prosperous. Jealous rivals managed to drive him out after five years, however, and he returned to a life of teaching. As an older man, he finally secured another, lesser position in a different province where he served until his death.

Neither Confucius nor his ideas were widely known at that time. Seventy of his disciples wrote down his teachings and spread them throughout China. They also wrote commentaries and expanded on his teachings. Within a century of his death, his ideas were known all over China. Knowledge of his writings and principles became a standard part of the educational system. The best-known of his disciples was Mencius, born about a hundred years after Confucius died. The *Book of Mencius* elaborates on Confucius's original teaching and adds some of his own ideas.

The core of Confucian teaching concerned proper relationships and reciprocal obligations. He spoke much about *li,* a Chinese word usually rendered "propriety." Li was the outward component of his teaching; its inward counterpart was *jen,* "goodness." Jen, he thought, was very rare and could only come from within, while li could be encouraged or even enforced through the right structures. Confucius, and Mencius after him, believed man was basically disposed to do good if the right conditions existed. To them, this meant a strong government with appropriate order and benevolent rulers. He believed a perfect society would result when key relationship pairs showed correct behavior toward each other. Those he identified as most important are:

1. Father to son (kindness from father/piety from son [*filial piety*])
2. Elder brother to younger brother (gentility from elder/ humility from younger)

3. Husband to wife (righteous behavior from husband/obedience from wife)
4. Elder to junior (consideration from elder/deference from junior)
5. Ruler to subject (benevolence from ruler/loyalty from subject)

While Confucian teachings spread and came to be adopted as the basis for Chinese society in the centuries after his death, veneration of his spirit became more closely linked to traditional Chinese religion. Introduction of Mahayana Buddhism into China around AD 300 accelerated this process, since Confucius came to be looked upon as another "Enlightened One." From this it was a small step toward deification and worship. Although Confucius himself never claimed his writings came from inspiration, they came to be seen as having supernatural origins due to their great wisdom and impact on China.

An Extra Minute

According to his disciples, when Confucius was asked about what would happen in the next life, he replied, "We have not yet begun to understand this life. How can we even ask about the next?"

Taoism

Because Taoism and Confucianism are so opposite in philosophy and concept, they're commonly treated as separate religions. Also, combining them would result in a very lengthy chapter, so the usual custom has been followed here. This is somewhat artificial, however, since Chinese religion as it is actually practiced combines these along with ancient polytheistic religions, including ancestor veneration and Buddhism. This is a community religion, and a traditional temple in Taiwan or rural China frequently contains statues of Confucius, Lao-tzu, Buddha, and many traditional deities all together.

Taoism takes its name from the title of the book *Tao Te Ching*, "The Way of Nature." In modern slang we might call this philosophy "It is what it is." This brief work—its length is about the same as five chapters of this book—rivals the *Analects of Confucius* as the most influential literature in Chinese history. Only the Bible has been translated more times than the *Tao Te Ching*, and more than a thousand commentaries have been written about it.

The man traditionally credited with having written it and with starting Taoism was named Li-poh-yang, but he is better known by the title given him by his disciples, *Lao-tzu,* meaning "Old Master." In China, where age is highly revered, this title of respect even gave rise to a legend that he was born old. There is less historical information about Lao-tzu than any other founder of a world religion. Some scholars even doubt that this historical person ever existed. Confucian sources say he was born about 500 BC, and that the two shapers of Chinese life met in person. Many literary scholars believe the *Tao Te Ching* was compiled from multiple sources over several centuries.

Like Confucius, Lao-tzu and his early disciples were indifferent to the existence of gods and goddesses. His focus was on this life, and he made no appeal to a supernatural authority for rewarding good deeds or punishing bad ones. He believed good behavior was its own sufficient reward. In contrast to Confucius, however, Lao-tzu thought human effort, especially elaborate government structures, was useless. Rather, he advocated an approach to life we might call "actionless action." The reasoning was based on belief in a mysterious, universal force called the *Tao.* Although usually translated as "the Way" or "the Way of Nature," Lao-tzu taught that the Tao was indefinable. He said, "The Tao that can be told of is not an Unvarying Tao." The Tao is not a god and has no personality that can be worshiped or prayed to—it's the Taoist conception of ultimate reality. The most oft-used analogy is a river, which flows unstoppably with a current that over time wears away even the hardest stone. Therefore, the goal of life is to live and move in harmony with the Tao, or as we might say today, to "go with the flow."

In practical terms, this meant life was the greatest gift of the Tao and that it should be lived simply, with as little moving against the current as possible. Some Taoists abandoned education, government positions, even their families in search of simplicity. Simplicity also was thought to be the way to prolong life; long life was valued above all else. Later Taoism moved beyond approaches to healthy living and began to use magical arts to prolong life.

The original form of Taoism, never popular with the masses, was devoid of any religious ceremony. But early in the first millennium AD, significant changes began to emerge. By AD 500, Taoism was the name given to what was likely the most popular religion in China. Internally, Taoists had moved the quest for long life beyond simple living and diet to magic, and then alchemy. From this it was no big step, given Chinese polytheism, to add gods, sacrifices, and prayers. Shrines became temples; sacrifices and prayers became rituals; increasing complexity necessitated specialists who knew the ceremonies and how to conduct them. A professional priesthood developed.

When mixed with the older Chinese religions, desire to know the correct way became elaborate forms of divination. In some cases, séances were held to ask departed ancestors for guidance. In its simpler form, a common approach still in use is oracle blocks. These carved pairs of woodblocks are prayed over, usually in a temple, and then tossed on the ground. It's a religious coin-flip of sorts, the position of the blocks giving a yes/no answer to questions.

The early Taoists had been pacifists, not on moral grounds, but rather because "going with the flow" meant accepting whatever the Tao brought, including invading armies, which were not to be resisted. Later Taoist leaders, however, became generals of huge armies that sometimes sought to force Taoist principles on Chinese provinces.

Externally, the arrival of Mahayana Buddhism, around AD 300, was met initially with interest and acceptance. But opposition to the imported religion emerged, especially after Buddhist leaders tried to convince Chinese rulers to suppress and outlaw

Taoist religious practices. For several centuries, Taoism, Confucianism, and Buddhism traded places in ongoing competition for the favor of China's emperors and governors. Eventually, syncretism brought the three together, along with older religious practices. While some individuals still espouse one philosophical view, for the past thousand years all three have shared the religious landscape of traditional China, Taiwan, and the Chinese diaspora. Although Communist rule in China since 1949 has significantly reduced traditional religious practice, it survives in the country's rural areas.

An Extra Minute

According to a popular legend, in his quest for simplicity, Lao-tzu decided to leave China. When he reached a gate in the Great Wall, a guard recognized him and prevented him from passing until he had written down all his wisdom. Lao-tzu sat down, wrote the *Tao Te Ching*, was allowed to pass through, and was never heard from again.

Shinto

Shinto, Japan's traditional religion, combines animistic aspects with ancestor veneration. There are shrines, priests, and corporate ceremonies, but much of Shinto is practiced in the home. It has no founder or starting date and has been practiced in Japan since before recorded history. It is so imbedded in the culture that it didn't even have a name until the arrival of Confucianism, Buddhism, and Taoism from China in about AD 400, when it was called Shinto to distinguish it from the other systems. The name comes from the Chinese words *shen* and *tao*, meaning "the way of the gods." The Japanese name, *kami no michi*, means the same.

Although *kami* is usually rendered "gods," it has a much broader meaning in the Japanese mind. It refers not only to major deities like the Sun Goddess but also to lesser deities, spirits of ancestors, even a spiritual presence in trees or hills. Basically, anything possessing a form of spiritual power or influence fits into the category. The Japanese estimate there are eight million *kami*.

Shinto also has nationalistic aspects. Its mythology explains the origins of the Sun Goddess (Amaterasu), the creation of

Japan and the rest of the world, and how the Japanese emperors descended from Amaterasu, which is why they were believed by the Japanese to have divine status. In the 1930s, the military manipulated these traditions to justify the invasion of China and the attack on Pearl Harbor in 1941.

China's culture was much more advanced than Japan's when it brought Confucianism, Taoism, and Buddhism to the islands. This brought initial acceptance of the new religions, but also triggered other cultural and religious changes. Perhaps the most significant was adoption of the Chinese writing system; previously the Japanese language was unwritten. Shinto has no scriptures or inspired writings, but traditionalists used this new tool to record much of the ancient mythology in the *Kojiki*, a book of ancient events, thus establishing the legitimacy of Shinto among the newer imports.

Confucian and Taoist philosophy influenced Japanese culture in many ways, but religiously Buddhism, particularly its Mahayana form, eclipsed the others. There were periods of rejection and even persecution, but persistent Chinese and Korean missionaries eventually established Buddhism firmly in Japan (much syncretized with Shinto). In return, Japan developed new and unique forms of Buddhism, such as Zen and Tendai, which found their way back into China. This has not always been a happy alliance, with periods of competition and times of increased syncretism. Christianity also entered Japan around 1550 and won many followers.

A new political regime in AD 1600 revived Shinto and made it the state religion, along with government funding for its shrines and priests. This began an era of increasing Japanese nationalism and isolation from the rest of the world. Persecution of foreign religions escalated; Buddhists suffered, and tens of thousands of Christians were executed when they refused to renounce their faith. State support for Shinto ended in 1945 as one of the surrender demands at the end of World War II.

This historical background has produced an interesting religious phenomenon in Japan today. Christianity was reintroduced into Japan after 1860, but Christians are still less than 1 percent of the population. Recently, 80 million Japanese claimed to profess Shinto and 80 million said they were Buddhist. However, Japan's population was only 120 million at the time! (and, only 31 percent claim to have any religious faith).

Clearly, many Japanese are comfortable seeing themselves as both Shinto and Buddhist without really believing in any religion. To some extent, this is due to the different roles the two faiths play. While both have dedicated followers, many Japanese see Shinto more as a part of their culture than a formal religion. Shinto practices are part of being Japanese. Buddhism is seen as the formal religion. Because Shinto has no clear teaching on what happens after death, Buddhist rituals are often used when someone dies. In recent years, some cultural aspects of Christianity have become popular, and it's not uncommon now for a Japanese family to have a "Christian" wedding, a Shinto baby dedication, and a Buddhist funeral.

According to Shinto, humans are born good, and life is good. Death is bad, and is typically dealt with by Buddhism. While Japanese culture has strong standards for behavior, Shinto has no moral code in the sense of eternal reward or punishment. The spirits of deceased ancestors become *kami,* at least for a time, and are remembered through prayers and food or drink offerings. Because of Buddhist influence, many Japanese also believe in reincarnation.

An Extra Minute

The graceful, upwardly curving arch called a *torii* is the classic symbol of Japan. In the 1990s, a group of Shinto priests came to the mountains of Oregon to select some trees for the construction of a large torii. The trees needed not only to be the correct size, height, and grain, but likewise have the proper quality of kami. After the chosen trees were chained to a freighter's deck for the trip, a huge Pacific storm washed the logs off the deck, and the process had to be repeated.

Secular Humanism

Secular Humanism is not merely nontheistic. It is zealously anti-theistic. Secular Humanists hold that belief in God is the greatest danger humanity faces, and human "salvation" requires total elimination of belief in the supernatural.

So why include it in a book on world religions? As noted in chapter 1, Secular Humanism fits our working definition of religion as an organized system of beliefs that answers ultimate questions about life. It has councils and associations, conferences and workshops, and a statement of beliefs. As we've seen, many belief systems are not based on belief in or reliance on the supernatural. Theravada Buddhism, Jainism, and Confucianism, for instance, believe the answers come from within, not from any source beyond humanity. The inclusion of Secular Humanism is consistent, and besides, it would be strange to ignore a belief system that has the stated goal of eradicating the beliefs and practices described in every other chapter of this book.

Secular Humanism's foundation is built on the philosophy of naturalism, or materialism: that the material universe (the natural world) is all that exists. This it shares with atheism, the belief that there is sufficient evidence to deny the existence of God and the supernatural. Agnostics, those who say there is insufficient evidence to know whether God (or the supernatural) exists, may also embrace Secular Humanism. But for Secular Humanists, atheism is just a beginning point. They have developed a complete worldview and value system built on naturalistic presuppositions.

As an organized system it differs from *secularism*, a much broader term referring to the worldview of those who live as if God does not exist. This includes all the nonreligious, estimated by researcher David Barrett to exceed 20 percent of earth's population. Certainly, Secular Humanism influences secular beliefs, but it goes beyond passively ignoring God to actively building a lifestyle and worldview based on opposition to belief in God.

Secular Humanism even goes beyond answers to ultimate life questions. It also seeks to apply those answers by promoting values without connection to any deity as their authority. According to the website of the Council for Secular Humanism,

> Atheism and agnosticism are silent on larger questions of values and meaning. If Meaning in life is not ordained from on high, what small-m meanings can we work out among ourselves? If eternal life is an illusion, how can we make the most of our only lives? As social beings sharing a godless world, how should we coexist?
>
> For the questions that remain unanswered after we've cleared our minds of gods and souls and spirits, many atheists, agnostics, skeptics, and freethinkers turn to secular humanism. (http.// secularhumanism.org/ [04/18/12])

Secular Humanism sees its roots in some ancient Greek and Roman philosophers, but its current form in the West is more directly connected to the Enlightenment. In the struggle between science and religion to claim the role of ultimate authority, humanists trusted human reason above all, though most still believed in the existence of God (usually in a deistic form). Publication of Charles Darwin's *On the Origin of Species* (1859) gave the humanists an explanation for human origins that didn't require God's existence, and the split was complete. A completely secular form of humanism began to grow.

In the public realm, Secular Humanists have had influence that far outweighs their numbers. Although it shares atheism and an antipathy against religion with Marxism, Secular Humanism distances itself from historical Communism and favors a democratic political system. Ironically, when the United States was founded, separation of church and state was a Christian idea, as Christians in Europe had faced persecution from their governments when their form of belief differed from that of the state church. But Secular Humanists now have turned this principle of non-coercion into the removal of any expression of religious beliefs, even historical ones, from the public arena. One example is the teaching of evolutionary theory to the exclusion of all other views as the answer to life's origins. The Council for Secular Humanism and its affiliate organizations frequently bring lawsuits against schools and local governments over anything they construe as religious expression.

Their beliefs are outlined in the "Secular Humanist Declaration" (1980), which was preceded by two earlier documents. Humanist Manifesto I was published in 1933 (after some years in the making), but lacking knowledge of later scientific discoveries, it assumed evolution was a somewhat rapid process and that humans had nearly achieved an almost utopian progress. This was consistent with the general post–WWI ("War to End All Wars") optimism. However, World War II and the ensuing Cold War made this manifesto seem somewhat naïve and simplistic. In 1973, it was replaced with Humanist Manifesto II, which asserted the need for a more aggressive approach to eliminating religion rather than waiting for evolution to finish the job. It, too, had its weaknesses and was soon replaced by the later Secular Humanist Declaration.

The Secular Humanist worldview certainly is not without flaws. Charles Darwin's views on human evolution were the basis for many forms of overt racial discrimination (such as the eugenics movement) and the "scientific" justification for Hitler's concept of the "master race" that led to the Holocaust. This is not to say, however, that current Secular Humanists support such views, even though the underlying worldview assumptions remain unchanged.

An Extra Minute

One trait of Secular Humanism, though not unique in this respect, is its frequent use of straw-man arguments in attacks upon believers. This is obvious in reading the Secular Humanist Declaration and the statements of Secular Humanist writers. The late renowned Christopher Hitchens characterized those who believe in God as people who favor "thuggish, tribal human designs" (while materialists are opposed).

Cults, "Isms," and Contemporary Religious Movements

The last chapters of this book deal with belief systems not typically categorized as world religions, even though some of them are global in nature and have many millions of followers. The number of adherents to Mormonism (The Church of Jesus Christ of Latter-day Saints), for instance, far exceeds the number of adherents to Judaism, Jainism, or Baha'i, and Mormons are in nearly every country though usually categorized as a cult. Conversely, Sikhism is small in numbers and followed by just one ethnic group (though it has spread somewhat through migration), but is nearly always found in books on world religions. How do we distinguish a cult from a religion?

At the outset, we must know there is no "Central Board of Religions" that decides what "gets in" and what doesn't. Some books include Baha'i and some don't. Some books on contemporary religious movements include it as well, just as most would include the Nation of Islam. (This book places that organization after the chapters on Islam just because that's where most readers might expect to find it due to its relationship to orthodox Islam.)

By our working definition (see chapter 1), all these are religions—organized sets of beliefs that answer ultimate questions. So how does one end up as a religion and another as a contemporary religious movement? Some criteria do help distinguish one from another. A few belief systems are rather obviously one or the other. With some we might make the case either way.

The *Oxford English Dictionary* defines a cult as "a relatively small group of people having beliefs or practices regarded by others as strange or as imposing excessive control over members." In this sense, cults were regarded as breakaway groups from established religions that held beliefs not accepted by the original faith. A cult, then, was a non-orthodox version of another religion that claimed to be the correct version. Jehovah's Witnesses and Mormons both claim to be *the* true followers of the Bible. Ahmadiyyas and the Nation of Islam both claim to be the correct version of Islam, even as they hold beliefs unacceptable to orthodox Muslims and contrary to the Qur'an.

But this explanation doesn't work for many other belief systems usually labeled cults. Hare Krishna is considered a Hindu cult, yet because it accepts reincarnation and karma, most mainstream Hindus consider it an orthodox branch. Baha'i, once considered a Muslim cult, now more often is regarded as a separate religion in its own right. And Mormons can scarcely be called "a relatively small group of people."

Further, the above definition fails to help us understand or categorize belief systems like Scientology or Wicca. While these and other faiths share some beliefs with long-established faiths, they are not closely tied to any of the world religions. One thing that does characterize all these belief systems, however, is that they are relatively new. Some may have older roots, but none began in an organized form earlier than 1800, and many are twentieth-century phenomena. The more common term these days is *contemporary religious movements* (CRMs) or *new religious movements* (NRMs).

Some would say, with Solomon, "There is nothing new under the sun" (Ecclesiastes 1:9). On the plane of core beliefs this is true. There are historical examples of religions upholding monotheism, polytheism, pantheism, atheism, and deism. No new system has come up with anything at that level not seen before.

But they do yield new combinations and appear in new locations. Transcendental Meditation is most popular in the West, which long had minimal if any exposure to the Hindu philosophy that lies at its foundation. And while many such systems draw their beliefs from older religions, another characteristic of most is that they began in the United States.

Modern technology has helped the spread of these movements. The Internet makes international access possible for anyone who buys a domain name and has basic design skills. All the same, all religions use technology, and utilizing newer media isn't in any sense unique to newer belief systems.

Undoubtedly, some will disagree with the choices made for this book. Given the number of new religious movements today, that is to be expected. It would be impossible to include them all even if this were a much longer work. But some common examples are found in the following chapters, and plenty of resources are available with more information.

An Extra Minute

This book considers theology rather than sociology in choosing which CRMs to include. Seventh-Day Adventism, for example, is not included since that movement, though it has cult-like origins, does not deny orthodox Christian teaching. Nothing in the Bible says one cannot be vegetarian or that we must worship on Sunday rather than Saturday. It is possible to be different and still within the bounds of a religion's scriptural teachings/ accepted beliefs.

The Unitarian-Universalist Association, The Unity School of Christianity, and The Unification Church

These three belief systems are considered in one chapter not because they are necessarily similar in belief but because the similarity of their names sometimes has led to confusion. We'll look at each separately.

The Unitarian-Universalist Association formed from the 1959 merger of the Unitarian Church and Universalism, which, historically, developed separately. Unitarian beliefs have roots in the anti-Trinitarian controversies of Christianity's early centuries but came into their present form during the Enlightenment. Unitarianism found greatest growth and popularity in the U.S., particularly through the speaking and writing of the nineteenth-century essayist Ralph Waldo Emerson. In contrast to orthodox Christian teaching, Unitarians follow the ethics of Jesus but deny his divinity. They believe the apostle Paul was the one who intentionally elevated Jesus' standing—that Jesus himself was strictly human and knew it. Unitarianism was and remains popular chiefly with the intelligentsia.

Universalism had like beginnings and, as with Unitarianism, found the height of its popularity in nineteenth-century New England, in large part a reaction against the strict Puritan form of Calvinism prevalent in that period. In addition to rejecting Jesus as divine or as Messiah, it also saw hope for salvation in other religions. Following the 1959 merger, Unitarians also adopted this idea.

The association's statement of purpose declares their sources of tradition as being found in the wisdom of the world's religions, Jewish and Christian teachings, and humanist counsel, among others. It understands salvation not in terms of heaven or hell but in the betterment of the human spirit and evil's removal from the world. Their emphasis mostly is on social issues. In 1985, they claimed about 175,000 members and over a thousand congregations.

Charles and Myrtle Fillmore founded The Unity School of Christianity in 1889. Charles was interested in Eastern religions and the occult. Myrtle, his wife, was a follower of Christian Science; this mix came together in Unity.

Although Unity makes extensive use of biblical vocabulary, its basic belief system is more like Hinduism. God is the source of everything but is not distinct from the human soul. As with Christian Science, Jesus was only human; Christ was just the spiritual aspect of him. "Jesus was potentially perfect and He expressed that perfection; we are potentially perfect and we have not expressed it," according to Unity writings. The focus is on health, spiritual healing, and prosperity. All of us have Christ

147

potential within us. The goal of Unity is to replace the physical human body with a true spiritual body through a series of reincarnations, so that everyone becomes a Christ.

Unity has been more successful numerically than its Christian Science parent (see chapter 35). The Silent Unity staff at the Unity Village center in Kansas City fields tens of thousands of calls and many more letters annually, offering prayer, counsel, and literature. The *Handbook of Denominations in the United States* says each year it publishes two hundred million magazines, books, booklets, and tracts. Unity markets itself as an educational system yet does have an underlying theology—it trains and ordains ministers and maintains congregations around the U.S.

Since the deaths of Myrtle (1931) and Charles (1948), their sons and a grandson have led the organization. Total membership nationally, plus the many international affiliates, is estimated at one million.

The Rev. Sun Myung Moon founded The Unification Church, in 1954, as The Holy Spirit Association for the Unification of World Christianity. Its followers, commonly called "Moonies," currently number about ten thousand in the U.S., though there were more at Unification's peak in the 1980s. Moon was born in 1920 in what is now part of North Korea, and later moved to South Korea. In 1972, he moved to the U.S., where he lived until recently reclaiming South Korea as his primary residence.

Even as a child, Moon had spiritualistic tendencies. He says that at age sixteen he had a vision of Jesus, who said to complete the task he (Jesus) had left undone. He was later influenced by a fringe group claiming the future Messiah would be Korean-born. Moon has not publicly announced himself as such, but his followers clearly believe he is that Messiah.

In 1957, Moon published the *Divine Principle*, which became the basis for Unification doctrine. In it he describes three theological "Ages": the Old Testament, the New Testament, and the Completed. The *Divine Principle* serves as the scripture for this final Age. Allegedly, the crucifixion was an untimely accident, occurring before Jesus was able to marry and produce children. Thus, he failed to right the wrongs of the first Adam (and Eve), and so there is a need for a third Adam to complete the process. Christ's resurrection was only spiritual and, as a result, accomplished only spiritual redemption.

It remains to the third Adam to provide physical redemption. Although he has not publicly said he is the third Adam, after several divorces, Moon declared his fourth wife, Hak Ja Han, to be the second Eve and "perfect mother." Hell is the present earth, which one day will be replaced by the kingdom of God—which the third Adam will usher in.

Sun Myung Moon had already become a wealthy businessman before moving to the U.S., where he established or purchased additional companies, including the *Washington Times*. He or the Unification Church also have founded nearly a dozen nonprofit religious or political organizations, including the American Freedom Coalition, which lobbies for and financially supports conservative and anti-Communist issues.

An Extra Minute

The Rev. Sun Myung Moon is best known in the U.S. for a mass service at Madison Square Garden, in 1982, in which he married more than two thousand couples. Moon had matched them from among his followers (who were mostly young and single); many had known each other less than a month. A Canadian newspaper claimed he officiated at a 1988 ceremony in which 6,500 couples were wed. In a South Korean stadium, Moon offered a wedding blessing for 300,000 couples, in 1992, and another 360,000 couples in 1995.

Christian Science
and Scientology

O nce again, we'll look at different faith systems with similar names in one chapter, since sometimes these also are
confused with each other.

The Church of Christ, Scientist is the official name of a move-
ment (founded in 1879 by Mary Baker Eddy) commonly referred
to as Christian Science. The name is well known through the
Christian Science Monitor, a respected newspaper, and through
Christian Science Reading Rooms in major cities around the
U.S. and in other countries.

Christian Scientists claim to be one of Christianity's denominations, with a faith based on the Bible. Indeed, their literature and official website contain frequent scriptural quotations,
usually from the King James Version. Their interpretations,
however, and their answers to ultimate questions, show a belief

system substantially different from orthodox Christianity of any branch or denomination.

Christian Science tenets are based on the teachings and writings of Mary Baker Eddy (1821–1910), who dealt with many illnesses during her childhood and early adult life, and spent much time and energy seeking and trying cures. In 1862, she met and was treated by Phineas Parkhurst Quimby, whose "Science of Man" theory promoted a concept of mental healing. She claimed healing by his approach and began to write of her studies and experiences.

In 1875, Eddy published *Science and Health with Key to the Scriptures*, which remains the basis of Christian Science belief. In 1879, she founded the Church of Christ, Scientist in Boston, later called the Mother Church, which is the Christian Science headquarters to this day. She also composed a number of additional works before her death.

In opposition to the Christian view of the material universe as God's real creation, Eddy taught that the material world is illusory. Only spirit is real, true, and infinite. While this sounds similar to monistic Hinduism, there is no evidence Eddy had any contact with Hindu thinking. Her beliefs also bear some resemblance to Greek dualism, in which matter is evil and spirit is good and pure. (Jainism holds this same view, independently of ancient philosophy.)

Combining this view with an emphasis on healing, Christian Science understands illness as errant belief in the reality of the physical. Prayer and focusing on right belief are keys to health and well-being. On the Christian Science website, a member shares the following testimony about how he dealt with an injury suffered in a baseball game: "On the way (I was able to drive) I prayed for myself, which is what I normally do in these types of situations. I asserted that my true being was spiritual, not material, and that I existed in God, where no accident had ever occurred. I knew that all physical evidence to the contrary was just the suggestion of the carnal mind that I possessed a material body and was therefore vulnerable to injury" (http:// christianscience.com/prayer-and-health/inspiration/publications /the-christian-science-journal/card-carrying-christian-scientist [04-18-12]).

Christian Science uses the words *God, Life, Love,* and *Truth* more or less interchangeably. As God is spirit, God is everything that is good and perfect. It also differentiates between the human Jesus and Christ, who is the spiritual power of God. Jesus was mortal and, since the material isn't real, merely an idea. But his life showed us Christ, the "divine idea of God."

Humanity's relationship with God also hints at monism. While not overtly saying humans actually are God, an oft-used Christian Science saying is "I am the place where God shines through, for God and I are one, not two."

In addition to the Mother Church, First Church of Christ, Scientist in Boston, there are branch churches across the U.S. and in approximately seventy other countries. Services include hymns and prayers, but there is no sermon. Christian Scientists refer to *Science and Health with Key to the Scriptures* and the Bible as their "pastor." Elected lay readers read portions from Eddy's writings and the Bible. These readings are the same worldwide, following a schedule determined by Mother Church leadership. Although there is no clergy in the usual sense, Christian Science practitioners are trained to teach Christian Science doctrine and help people pray for physical healing.

Scientology, widely known for the celebrities among its members, was started by L. Ron Hubbard (1911–1986) in 1955. A moderately successful science-fiction author, Hubbard said, in 1949, "Writing for a penny a word is ridiculous. If a man really wants to make a million dollars, the best way would be to start his own religion." Using his 1950 bestseller *Dianetics: The Modern Science of Mental Health* as a foundation, that's exactly what he did.

Scientology combines pop psychology and an eclectic mix of theology into one system. It teaches that human beings were once thetans, godlike creatures who gave up their powers to enter MEST (matter, energy, space, time). Scientology's goal is to help humans recover the power of deity that lies hidden within them. The method is the removal of engrams, which reside below the conscious level in the reactive side of the brain and are the result of traumatic past experiences. When all engrams are removed, a person becomes a Clear. Scientology offers a number of courses to assist people in becoming Clears. Advanced courses guide Clears to become OTs, or Operating Thetans. The entire process of becoming a Clear and achieving all nine OT stages can cost over a hundred thousand dollars.

Scientology is polytheistic and, along with embracing reincarnation, is casual with regard to other religions. Hubbard said that "neither Lord Buddha nor Jesus Christ were OTs according to evidence. They were just a shade above Clear" (*Certainty* magazine [5:10]). From its headquarters in southern California, Scientology recently has tried to remarket itself as a science rather than a religion.

An Extra Minute

In 1989, the head of the U.S. Consulate in Mombasa, Kenya, contracted malaria. As a member of the Church of Christ, Scientist, she refused medical treatment. When the consul's condition deteriorated to where she was incapacitated and nearly comatose, the U.S. government hospitalized her, started treatment, and she began to recover. Then her sister (also a follower of Christian Science) arrived, insisted treatment be stopped, and removed the consul from the hospital. She died two days later.

Mormonism

The Church of Jesus Christ of Latter-day Saints, often called the Mormon (or LDS) Church, is probably the best known and undoubtedly the largest of the religious movements begun since 1800. Since 1950, it has doubled in size every fifteen years, and in 2010, claimed fourteen million members worldwide, with over half that membership outside the U.S. Much of its growth is attributable to its missionary program: Tens of thousands of clean-shaven, white-shirt-and-tie-clad young men give two years of their life, at their own or their family's expense, to spread the LDS Church's message globally. In an average twenty-four-month stint a missionary converts five people to the Mormon faith.

Once found mainly in Utah, Mormons now live in all fifty states and nearly every nation. Formerly despised, on the fringe of society, Mormons have become a mainstream group. They head large corporations like Marriott and Albertsons and are elected as representatives and senators—there's even a chance that by the time you read this a Mormon will be working out of the Oval Office. Their strong family values help them find acceptance in almost every neighborhood. Many Americans, including some members of the LDS Church, assume they're another Christian denomination. But their actual teaching contradicts Christianity on a number of key points. Mormon use of Christian terms, with different meanings, causes and spreads confusion.

The Mormon Church was founded with six members in Fayette, New York, on April 6, 1830. Its founder, Joseph Smith Jr., said God had revealed to him that none of the Christian denominations was the correct one and that he was to restore the true faith. Smith claimed a number of revelations through appearances by divine messengers. The one appearing most often was Moroni, a glorified being and the son of an ancient prophet named Mormon.

Among other messages, Moroni told Joseph Smith where some metal plates had been buried in the woods. Smith's translation of these plates is the *Book of Mormon*, which along with *Doctrine and Covenants* and *Pearl of Great Price*, added later, became the primary Mormon scriptures. Smith claimed the plates were written in "Reformed Egyptian" hieroglyphics (a nonexistent language). He also said that upon complete translation, Moroni took the plates to heaven (so there is no way to verify his claim). Mormons also claim to follow the Bible "as far as it is translated correctly" (8th Article of Faith). "Correct" is anything that does not contradict the other books, so in practice Smith's revelations hold authority over the Bible. Prophets of the LDS Church can add (and have added) further revelations.

The fledgling group grew rapidly and made moves due to friction with non-Mormons (whom LDS members call Gentiles). They settled in Ohio, briefly, then two locations in Missouri, followed by Commerce, Illinois, which they renamed Nauvoo (Smith said this was Hebrew for "Beautiful Place"). During this period, Smith claimed more revelations and wrote more scriptures, supplementing his original teaching, and announced his candidacy for U.S. president. Continued friction with non-Mormons, controversy over polygamy, and Smith's destruction of a non-Mormon newspaper office led to his arrest in 1844. On June 27, a mob stormed the jail and killed Joseph Smith and his brother Hyrum.

Following Smith's death, the Mormon community divided. The largest group followed Brigham Young on a famous journey west to the Salt Lake Valley in present-day Utah. The largest of several splinter groups accepted Smith's son, Joseph Smith III, as prophet and leader. Staying in the Midwest, they officially registered, in 1860, as the Reorganized Church of Jesus Christ of Latter-day Saints. They use Smith's own Bible translation rather than the King James Version used by Young's group. Their headquarters is in Independence, Missouri. In 2001, they changed their name to the Community of Christ.

As the main group continued to grow, it faced a number of challenges. Brigham Young had announced, in 1852, a previously secret revelation of Joseph Smith's promoting the importance of polygamy. Young himself had fifty-five wives. As Utah was seeking statehood, the LDS Church began to distance itself from the practice. An 1890 manifesto warned against plural marriages, and a 1904 edict strengthened that warning with excommunication against polygamous unions, though the practice still continues in splinter groups. In 1978, LDS President Spencer W. Kimball reversed the Mormon position on racial issues. Joseph Smith had taught that black skin was a curse and prohibited African-Americans from holding the priesthood. Since this change, the LDS Church has experienced rapid growth in Africa.

Mormon doctrine teaches that there are many gods and that God the Father is god only of this world. The gods were once humans who achieved a glorified status, which is taught in the couplet "As man is, God once was; as God is, man may become." The goal of Mormonism is ultimately to become a god of one's own world. In heaven, a Heavenly Father and Mother produce spirit children who await bodies so they can become human and begin the process (this is the main reason Mormons typically have large families).

Jesus, the first of God the Father's spiritual children, became a human through physical relationship between God the Father and a human mother. His death purchased resurrection for all people, who will face a judgment and spend eternity in one of four places. The celestial kingdom is for those who accept Mormon doctrine. The terrestrial kingdom is for good people who reject Mormon teaching on earth but later accept it in the spirit world. The telestial kingdom is for those who twice reject Mormon doctrine. The outer darkness is for Satan, his angels, and former Mormons who left the Church.

The celestial kingdom itself contains three levels. To attain the highest level, a necessity to eventual godhood, one must accept Mormon doctrine *and* carry out numerous temple rituals. For most of LDS Church history, there was only one temple, first in Ohio when the group settled there, then rebuilt in Salt Lake City. More recently, as Mormonism has grown significantly, more temples have been built in major cities across the U.S. and overseas. Rituals like eternal marriages and baptisms for the dead are carried out in the temples. (There are many additional rituals for the leadership.)

An Extra Minute

As the LDS Church continues to expand and become more generally accepted, it may see further revelations from leadership that further change controversial teachings. Core beliefs, however, will remain the same. Many, from those who have accepted an invitation to attend a Mormon church, to those who have married into a Mormon family, know little or nothing about LDS doctrine and assume it is a variation of Christianity.

Jehovah's Witnesses

Jehovah's Witnesses are well known for the door-to-door pairs who encourage people to join Bible studies and purchase Watchtower literature. They have produced more than thirty billion pieces of literature and spend over a billion hours annually distributing it. *The Watchtower* magazine is published in nearly two hundred languages and has a worldwide circulation that more than doubles that of *Reader's Digest.*

Jehovah's Witness theology is based on the writings of Charles Taze Russell (1852–1916), who, influenced by certain Adventist preachers as to the second coming of Christ, founded the *Zion's Watch Tower and Herald of Christ's Presence* magazine in 1879. He wrote articles teaching that Christ had returned invisibly in 1874 and would establish God's visible kingdom in 1914. Soon after, he established Zion's Watch Tower Tract Society, the forerunner of the current Watchtower Bible and Tract Society. As they do today, Russell's followers sold books, magazines, and other literature door to door. In 1904, he completed his six-volume *Studies in the Scriptures.*

Then 1914 passed without Russell's prophecies coming true, and he died in 1916. His successor was Joseph Rutherford, a prolific writer of nearly a hundred books and tracts. Rutherford taught that Christ's invisible return began, rather than ended, in 1914, and that God's kingdom would arrive in 1925. This also failed. When Rutherford died in 1942, his replacement was Nathan Knorr, best known for (1) his training programs for door-to-door work and (2) the *New World Translation* of the Bible, which "restored" the name *Jehovah* to the New Testament (*Jehovah* is based on an Old Testament Hebrew word, translated LORD in most English versions. It does not exist in Greek, the primary original New Testament language). The *New World Translation* also differs from recognized scholarship in altering the translation of passages that touch on the deity of Christ.

Even before Knorr's death, in 1977, major reorganization of the Watchtower Society and its entities occurred. Under his leadership, the Society had predicted Christ would return in 1975 and establish an earthly paradise. When this likewise failed, many Witnesses were disillusioned. A second restructuring followed in 2000, separating administrative duties from the "ministry of the word." Subsequent leaders have sought to downplay the setting of dates and create explanations for the "seeming" failure of previous prophecies.

Jehovah's Witnesses are discouraged from questioning their leaders' teachings. The Watchtower has admonished, "We should seek for dependent Bible study rather than for independent Bible study" (e.g., 09/15/11, 4885). Central to these teachings are that God the Father is Jehovah and that he, the only true God, must be referenced by this name alone. Jesus is a lesser god, created by Jehovah as the Archangel Michael; through him the world and everything else was created. The Trinity, therefore, is a false teaching with origins in ancient Babylonian theology. Jesus' earthly life was not an incarnation—his birth was as an ordinary human.

Thus his sacrificial death on the cross cancelled out Adam's sin but no one else's. Further, his resurrection was as an angelic spirit being, not with a glorified body. His bodily appearances to his disciples were in a temporary form, as angels can sometimes take on a temporary body. And finally, with regard to the nature of God, Jehovah's Witnesses teach that the Holy Spirit is an impersonal force (not the third person of the Trinity).

With regard to humanity, Jehovah's Witnesses speak of Christ's ransom as applying only to those who earn it through adherence to Watchtower doctrine and practices. Among the righteous are two classes of people. The "anointed class" numbers 144,000 (taken from Revelation 7:4). This group is variously described as either very righteous Witnesses who died before 1935, or who were already alive, even as infants, in 1918. The anointed class will rule in heaven with Christ. The "other sheep" (see John 10:16) are the rest of the faithful Witnesses. They will not go to heaven, but will live forever in an earthly paradise. Humans have no eternal spirit that lives on after physical death. The body simply lies in the grave until the resurrection. At Christ's return the dead are raised and the great battle of Armageddon takes place, followed by the Judgment. The anointed ones go to heaven, the other sheep go to the earthly paradise, and all the rest are annihilated and cease to exist.

Socially, the Jehovah's Witnesses face a number of challenges. They do not celebrate any holidays, religious or national, or even birthdays, since they view a holiday as giving honor to someone or something other than Jehovah. For the same reason, they refuse to salute the flag or say the Pledge of Allegiance. More controversially, Witnesses refuse to have blood transfusions, believing the Bible prohibits it. The Supreme Court ruled that religious conviction does not allow someone to refuse blood transfusion if it is court-ordered, but court intervention has been rare, and many have died in need of a transfusion.

An Extra Minute

The idea that the highest God created the universe through a lesser god is not new with Jehovah's Witnesses' teaching. The ancient Greeks believed spirit was pure, and flesh (the material world) was evil. In order to avoid contamination by proximity to material things, the high God created a lesser god through whom the world was created. This philosophy crept into some early Christian heresies as an attempt to explain how Jesus could still be "god" yet not equal to God the Father. The essential unity and equality of the Father, Son, and Spirit is well supported in Scripture, however, meaning that Jehovah's Witnesses are not (nor have they ever claimed to be) just another Christian denomination.

Neopagan Religions

T he Goddess is alive and magic is afoot." Thus proclaimed an I-694 billboard in a Minneapolis suburb a few years ago, sponsored by the Goddess Committee, Northern Dawn Council, Covenant of the Goddess. The growth of Neopagan religions in North America and Europe has been one of the most significant expressions of new religious movements since 1950. Many today use the word *pagan* to refer to nonreligious people or those whose behavior is considered unacceptable, but *Pagan* actually is an umbrella term for the ancient religions of pre-Christian Europe. These did not cease to exist after most Europeans converted, at least nominally, to Christianity, but they did go underground and were often viewed with suspicion, as they frequently are today. Neopagan religions are a revival and repackaging of these belief systems with some contemporary additions.

Wicca is the best known of this large family of contemporary religious movements, though there are many different groups. Druidism, Celtic religions, Asatru, the Green Circle, and the

Circle of Awen are a handful of the many examples. The variety makes generalizing difficult, but a few themes do characterize most. Neopagan religions view themselves as distinct from New Age religions, and outside observers typically agree. Neopagan religions are most closely related to the huge animistic family of belief systems; New Age religions usually draw their core beliefs from the Hindu worldview. But Neopagan religions typically express polytheistic beliefs rather than the deism of other animistic faiths.

Neopagan belief systems are usually described as "nature religions." Mother Earth or an earth Goddess is often the central deity or highest spiritual entity. Environmental issues are often highly important, as caring for the earth is a direct or indirect form of worship. And feminine centrality, while not intended to exclude men from religious participation, can be deliberately emphasized in opposition to male dominance in formal religions.

As Neopagan religions have grown in popularity, their followers have made an effort to distinguish and distance themselves from Satan worship. When Wiccans, for example, speak of witchcraft, they are thinking in terms of rituals that derive power from nature or spiritual forces in nature, not from Satan; think *Harry Potter* rather than *The Exorcist*. In fact, many Neopagan practitioners don't even believe in Satan's existence. This is a particularly sensitive area for many Neopagans, who view the witch trials of past centuries as misguided persecution of the Pagan nature religions. It is common for them to view themselves as survivors of a movement that predates Christianity and was nearly wiped out in the past.

In common with animistic religions, Neopagan religions make frequent use of rituals and symbols; pentagrams, circles, and objects in threes are common. As with other animistic belief systems, rituals are about developing or using spiritual power.

As a result, they are pragmatic, seeking what works. Wicca, for example, constantly develops new rituals as practitioners experiment with various methods.

Many Neopaganist forms make use of *magick*, intentionally spelled in the archaic form to distinguish it from modern illusionists, who use sleight of hand, visual distraction, and mechanical devices to produce "tricks." Magick is the use of rituals to produce physical outcomes through spiritual power. Telekinesis is a basic illustration. Use of magick to put curses on people is rare, as it's believed that whatever you do to others comes back to you thrice over. Wiccans follow an ethical principle that says, "And if it harm none, do what thou wilt." Nevertheless, it is recognized that a few witches do practice so-called "black magic," which is worked to bring harm to others.

In the dualism of most Neopagan religions, bad things are not "evil" but simply the necessary dark side of a good counterpoint. *Star Wars* popularized this idea with the two sides of The Force. This dualism does not mean, though, that there are no ethics in Neopaganism. It's just that the ethics are based on the "three times" retribution principle rather than on a revealed or absolute moral code.

Neopagan religions have little formal organization or central leadership; groups are generally local and fairly small. *Covens* of witches in Wicca are an example, although each belief system has a different name for its local groups. They also tend to be egalitarian in regard to leadership. Priests and priestesses have more skills but not necessarily more authority. Due to this characteristic, few Neopagan groups have formal belief statements. While there is a basic worldview behind the rituals, specific beliefs often are left to the individual.

Although many Neopagan rituals and practices are passed along orally, there is a growing number of written information sources. Aleister Crowley, a British writer, published several books that formed the basis for much of today's Neopagan beliefs and activities. Alexander Gardner's *Book of Shadows* has become a textbook of sorts for the Wiccan movement. Many other authors have produced fiction and nonfiction promoting Neopaganism.

Beliefs on life after death vary among Neopagan religions. Reincarnation is common but not universal, because of the cyclical aspect of nature. None believe in a final divine judgment or a permanent heaven and hell.

An Extra Minute

Because of Neopaganism's close connection with nature, many rituals and holidays are connected to cyclical natural events like solstices and equinoxes. Rituals typically begin in a "sacred space," invoke the four Guardians (earth, air, fire, and water), and follow with chanted liturgies and prayers.

New Age Religions

New Age is an umbrella term for a host of recent religious startups, most originating since 1970. The name comes from the expected dawning of a new age of human consciousness and development, often referred to as the Age of Aquarius from its connection to astrology. Although not original with her, Marilyn Ferguson's *The Aquarian Conspiracy*, considered by many the "bible" of New Age religions, did much to popularize the term.

There is no New Age "central headquarters" or mother organization. Most have developed independently of (sometimes in competition with) other, similar movements. They now exist in a vast network of autonomous groups held together by a few common beliefs.

New Age religions exhibit a wide variety of organizational variation as well. There are New Age churches with clergy, buildings, and regular services. Some practices, on the other hand, while based on the same core beliefs as other New Age faiths, may not seem connected to any particular organized religion at all. The use of crystals for physical healing and emotional improvement is one example. New Age books number in the thousands, and New Age bookstores everywhere in the West also offer products of many kinds to aid people in their quest for fulfillment. Shirley MacLaine's autobiographical works on reincarnation and other New Age topics have sold in the multimillions.

While there is tremendous variability in beliefs and practices, all may be characterized by the foundational belief that the answers to life problems lie within the person, not in any transcendent being or revealed scripture. This is connected to an underlying monistic worldview, adapted from Hinduism. There is no transcendent deity because we *all* are deities. The use of external tools (like crystals) or techniques are primarily to draw out the potential within us. In some cases, spirit guides may be sought through meditation or other techniques, but these are not "saviors" in any sense. With help, a person must achieve individual goals. According to New Age author Gary Zukav's *Soul Stories*, "Nonphysical teachers do not tell you what to do. They help you see your options. They help you think through choices. . . . Then you decide what to do" (36–37).

Something else that characterizes most New Age religions is belief in reincarnation and karma. Connected to this, again, is the necessity of finding one's own path to the goal, which may be called enlightenment, salvation, or unity with the divine (among other expressions). Reincarnation makes allowance for mistakes along the way, since one never needs to admit failure. If a person doesn't achieve the goal this time around, there will always be another opportunity to get it right.

Development of New Age religions came from profound disaffection with both formal, revealed religion—particularly Christianity—and Secular Humanism, which failed to provide answers for humanity's inner yearnings. During a time of cultural upheaval, the hippie movement, anti-Vietnam-War protests, and general rejection of traditional morality left many people seeking new answers to life's questions. Many looked to the East. While New Age religions usually reject Hindu deities and most practices, the majority share with Hinduism its world-view regarding the human soul and reincarnation. Some Buddhist beliefs also have found their way into New Age religions.

As New Age has grown and become more mainstream, it has shed its bell-bottomed, paisley-shirted image. Followers are more likely to be successful businesspeople in expensive suits. Ads for New Age products, once limited to specialty publications, now appear in regular media. Delta Airline's *Sky* magazine recently carried a full-page ad for the Q-Link, an acrylic pendant selling for $99.95 (or $259.95 in the executive, titanium version) and guaranteed to improve your energy and release your full potential while "shielding you from the harmful effects of EMF radiation."

At the same time, the language in which New Age beliefs and practices are communicated has recently changed. Former spirit mediums are now "channelers," or guides, or energies. Shamanistic practices (performed by those once known as witch doctors) are now "transformational therapies." Buddhist or Hindu forms of meditation are now "centering" or "grounding." While the terminology may be new, the underlying beliefs and most practices are based on ancient religious traditions.

One controversial change has been the widespread acceptance of yoga, now touted as stress-relieving exercise. Even some Christian churches host classes. Clothing and mats for yoga workouts are available everywhere. Christian and Muslim practitioners claim it is strictly physical exercise and has no religious connections. Others remain unconvinced. Yoga originally was a form of Hindu religious practice designed to allow a person closer communion with one's gods. Any physical benefit was at best secondary.

It's impossible to list all groups that might be considered New Age. A few actually use *New Age* in their names, most do not. The Vedanta Society and the Divine Light Mission are among the older groups, predating 1970. Scientology, Urantia, Arica, Eckankar, and The Forum (EST) are among the newer ones. Many initial organizations openly embraced Hindu thought and teaching. As the movement developed over the past four decades, it has outwardly distanced itself from its Hindu roots. Many of the newest forms make an effort to appear scientific or psychological rather than religious.

An Extra Minute

In his early days as Acharya Rajneesh, a correspondent once asked Osho (the current name for the late Bhagwan Shree Rajneesh) what his ten commandments were. In reply, he noted that it was difficult to say because he was against any kind of commandment, but "just for fun" he set out the following:

1. Never obey any command unless it is coming from within you also.
2. There is no God other than life itself.
3. Truth is within you; do not search for it elsewhere.
4. Love is prayer.
5. To become nothingness is the door to truth. Nothingness itself is the means, the goal, and attainment.
6. Life is now and here.
7. Live wakefully.
8. Do not swim—float.
9. Die each moment so that you can be new each moment.
10. Do not search. That which is, is. Stop and see.

40

Transcendental Meditation

Transcendental Meditation, popularly known as TM, typically would be considered a New Age religion (see chapter 39). For its size and popularity, it will be covered in a brief
chapter of its own.

The movement and related organizations were founded by
Maharishi Mahesh Yogi. He was born in northern India in 1917
(some sources say 1911, others 1918) and earned a university
degree in physics before renouncing worldly pursuits to become
a disciple of Swami Brahmananda Saraswati, better known as
Guru Dev. Following Guru Dev's death in 1953, Maharishi (a
Hindi title meaning "great seer") continued to meditate and
reflect, including two years spent in a Himalayan cave. These
meditations on Guru Dev's teachings became the basis for TM.

Maharishi Mahesh Yogi moved to the U.S. in 1958 and
founded the Spiritual Regeneration Movement in Los Angeles.
Although the initial response was small, the antiestablishment
mood of American youth in the later 1960s produced an interested audience for his message of peace and tranquility. The

Beatles began to follow him, even spending time at his *ashram* (meditation and training center) in India, and this publicity brought rapid growth. After a few years, there was a falling-out with the Beatles, especially John Lennon, who called Maharishi "a lecherous womanizer." (George Harrison continued to practice Hinduism; his former estate outside London is now a Hindu temple and retreat center.) The adverse publicity brought a decline in numbers, and in the early 1970s Maharishi returned to India.

But before long he was back in the U.S. He rebranded TM as the Science of Creative Intelligence (SCI), replacing all religious vocabulary with terms from psychology; the movement began to grow again. So great was the popularity of TM seminars (people paid $2,500 or more to attend) that in the 1970s, SCI was making up to $20 billion annually. In 1974, Maharishi bought the former Parsons College in Fairfield, Iowa, and founded the Maharishi International University. Through the university's research, TM sought to demonstrate the scientific basis of Transcendental Meditation, further distancing itself from allegations of religious teaching. For a time TM found its way into public schools, but in 1977, a federal court ruled that SCI/TM was indeed religion-based and banned it from being taught in New Jersey public schools. Some other states quickly adopted similar provisions, despite TM's loud and frequent protests.

This by no means brought an end to TM, which continues to advertise widely and grow through seminars offered all over the country. "I lowered my blood pressure naturally through TM," proclaims one advertisement, quoting the *American Journal of Cardiology*. It goes on, "Learn how Transcendental Meditation® can unfold perfect health and improve *your* quality of life." In a tacit admission of TM's religious basis, the fine print attributes the ad to the Maharishi Vedic Education Development Corporation.

The death of Maharishi Mahesh Yogi, in 2008, also did little to slow the growth of TM and its expanding number of related organizations. Currently, plans are in place to build Peace Palaces in three thousand major world cities. According to the website, "Each Peace Palace will offer to everyone the knowledge and practical programs for peace and enlightenment, for a healthy, happy, more creative, more fulfilling and successful life through the Transcendental Meditation program. Its benefits in the fields of education, health, social behavior, and world peace have been amply documented during the past half-century all over the world" (maharishipeacepalace.org [04/18/12]). Another organization, The Global Country of World Peace, aspires to assist current governments "by unifying all nations in happiness prosperity, invincibility, and perfect health" (www.globalcountry.org/wp/the-global-mother-divine-organization/ [04/18/12]). The administrators of various countries within the GCWP are called *rajas*. According to the Minneapolis *Star Tribune*, the cost of training to become a raja is $1 million. Rajas may have "vedic authority" over physically disparate political entities—Graham de Freitas, PhD, is raja of Minnesota, Norway, Grenada, Trinidad, and Tobago, and half a dozen African countries.

Transcendental Meditation itself is a procedure for reaching a state of "higher consciousness," releasing the practitioner's innermost potential. Unlike other forms of meditation, TM is supposed to transcend thinking. The basic techniques are taught in a seven-step course, currently costing $1,500. The Maharishi Foundation claims to have trained more than six million people worldwide over the past fifty years. Training includes giving the initiate a *mantra,* a word repeated while meditating. The primary requirement is relaxing while repeating the mantra for twenty minutes, twice daily. Advanced courses promise to move a person beyond transcendental consciousness to cosmic consciousness, God consciousness, and eventually unity consciousness, where one achieves complete unity with God and freedom from karma. These deeper levels show TM's connection to Hindu philosophy and worldview.

An Extra Minute

In July 2006, Professor John Hagelin, a theoretical physicist at the Maharishi University, began a yearlong experiment in bringing worldwide peace and prosperity through group meditation. The goal was to gather more than two thousand TMers to meditation twice a day for three hours each session. Expectations included an end to the war in Iraq and a rise in the Dow Jones Industrial Average. The DJIA was just over 11,000 in July 2006. By July 2007, it was almost 14,000. One year later it was back at 11,000 again.

Garry R. Morgan is Professor of Intercultural Studies at Northwestern College. He served with World Venture from 1974–1976 and 1982–1999 in Kenya, Ethiopia, Uganda, and Tanzania. Garry is married, has a grown daughter, and lives in the Minneapolis/St. Paul area.

Another User-Friendly Guide in 15 MINUTES A DAY

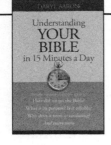

Whether you're a beginner or a seasoned reader, the Bible can be overwhelming at times. The short, digestible readings in this book dispel myths about where the Bible came from, what it is about, and why it matters. With its easy-to-navigate topical structure, this guide offers quick and clear answers to your most important questions about the bestselling book in history.

Understanding Your Bible in 15 Minutes a Day by Daryl Aaron

BET

sletters.